JIM CURRAN is a freelance cameraman [and] climber. He has climbed and filmed [on] documentaries (including the tragic eve[nts]) all the greats of the British mountaineering scene, including Chris Bonington, Joe Tasker, Alan Rouse, Joe Brown and Peter Boardman. He has also filmed in the Andes, Caucasus, Atlas Mountains, Tibet and China and, nearer home on the Old Man of Hoy and St Kilda.

His films and books have won many awards worldwide, and he has been shortlisted five times for the Boardman Tasker Award for Mountain Literature, and won the non-fiction award at the Banff Mountain Book Festival in 1996. He has also filmed, scripted and narrated the documentary *Rock Queen* with Catherine Destivelle, the French climbing superstar, which won him an Emmy Award for outstanding electronic camerawork. He is artistic director of the annual Kendal Mountain Film Festival.

He lives in Sheffield where his writing is constantly interrupted by the attractions of the Peak District in general, and of climbing on the gritstone outcrops in particular. He is the author of *High Achiever: The Life and Climbs of Chris Bonington*.

Praise for *The Middle-Aged Mountaineer*

'Jim [Curran] writes with a gentle self-deprecating humour that is never malicious . . . The illustrations add to the pleasure of the books . . . It is a very entertaining book by a climber who has done most of it, seen nearly all of it, who still loves it and can write about all of that and entertain you!'   Pip Hopkinson, *Climber*

'His characters are well-portrayed and there are wonderfully described anecdotes . . . *The Middle-Aged Mountaineer* offers compelling reading.'   Lindsay Griffin, *Activ Pursuits*

By the same author

THE
MIDDLE-AGED
MOUNTAINEER

Cycling and climbing the
length of Britain

JIM CURRAN

ROBINSON
London

Constable & Robinson Ltd
3 The Lanchesters
162 Fulham Palace Road
London W6 9ER
www.constablerobinson.com

First published in the UK by Constable,
an imprint of Constable & Robinson Ltd, 2001

This paperback edition published by Robinson,
an imprint of Constable & Robinson Ltd, 2003

A copy of the British Library Cataloguing in
Publication Data is available from the British Library

ISBN 1-84119-731-9 (pbk)
ISBN 1-84119-236-8 (hbk)

Printed and bound in the EU

10 9 8 7 6 5 4 3 2 1

Contents

Illustrations

Leaving home
The fully laden Beast
A bleak Shetland day
Catherine Destivelle on the top of the Old Man of Hoy
Catherine psyched up to solo the Old Man
Catherine on the long second pitch
Mike Banks on the crucial second pitch
Paul Nunn on Rangrik Rang
View across the Indian Himalaya to Kamet
The author approaching the overhang on Fionn Buttress†
Escaping the Highlands†
Cycling under the M1‡
The approach to Sheffield through the Rother Valley‡
Gemma making light work of Covent Garden, Millstone Edge§
Damp, cramped and fed up
Geoff Birtles nears the top of Land's End Long Climb*
Done it*

Photo credits:
† Terry Gifford
‡ Geoff Birtles
§ Ian Smith
* Ken Wrigley

All other images are author's own
All line drawings by author

Author's Note and Acknowledgements

This is the story of a long solo bicycle ride made in the wet summer of 2000. During the couple of months of cycling, I passed through some of the very best scenery that Britain can offer, scenery that has been part of my life for over forty years of climbing and walking. It proved to me, if proof were needed, that this tiny island can compete with anywhere in the world for natural beauty. There is still wilderness to be experienced, even if the hand of man is never far away. For me the journey was an affirmation of the wild country I have loved since, at the age of ten, I first went on holiday to Cornwall and was captivated by the sight of the cliffs at Kynance Cove and Gurnard's Head.

By an awful irony this book was made slightly easier to write as I, like everyone else, have been confined to barracks and almost completely deprived of my countryside fix due to the ravages of foot and mouth disease. Derbyshire, on my doorstep, is closed to walkers and climbers, though cyclists can still enjoy the views from the roads and it would still just about be possible to do the whole journey described in these pages. By the time these words appear in print I hope the restrictions will have become a memory. Meanwhile, as I write this celebration of British landscape, I do so knowing that the awful palls of smoke of burning sheep and cattle are drifting across Cumbria and Devon and much of the countryside is facing an uncertain future.

Although the bulk of the journey was made alone and unsupported, I relied along the way on the hospitality, help and encouragement of many old friends and some new ones. My most sincere thanks are due to my brother Philip and his partner Heather Miletto, Geoff and Jackie Birtles, Pip Hopkinson, Terry Gifford, Jim and Marcia Fotheringham, John and Rose Porter, Chris and Wendy Bonington, Nick and Jill Hopkinson, Ken

Wrigley, my daughters Becky and Gemma, Mike and Laraine Richardson, Rosemary and Fred Lapham, Cass Lane, Kay Dowling, Trevor Briggs and Denise Miller.

Before I even left Sheffield, I was helped by W. E. James Cycles Ltd, and for the umpteenth time by Berghaus Ltd where Sue Reay generously kitted me out with jacket, rucksack, boots and a pair of shorts I have never had the courage to wear. A particularly useful little article came from the office of the climbing magazine *High*. Called a buff, it is a tube of stretchy fabric which served as a scarf, a headband, a facemask, a towel and, I am ashamed to admit, a handkerchief during the hay fever season.

At Constable, Carol O'Brien has again shown that she has faith in me and down on the Gower peninsula my editor and friend Maggie Body has superintended my editorial gear ratios. The manuscript, which looked as if it had been written by a drunken spider, was deciphered and entered into electronic limbo at first by Serys O'Connor and later by Sue Evans who typed the bulk of it. Many, many thanks to both of you. Thanks are due to John Murray for permission to reprint 'Lullaby for Lucy' by George Mackay Brown. Thanks to *High* magazine and Geoff Birtles for permission to reproduce the article appearing in Chapter Eight, and to Terry Gifford for the poem contained in it. Also my thanks to David and Emma Briggs, my next door neighbours, for permission to reproduce my drawing of Black Slab, Stanage, which was their wedding present.

Finally of course, my heartfelt thanks must go to those to whom the book is dedicated: the Old Spice Girls – Hilary Nunn, Pam Beech, Pam Gleadall, Rita Davies and Sue Coonan.

Jim Curran, Sheffield
April 2001

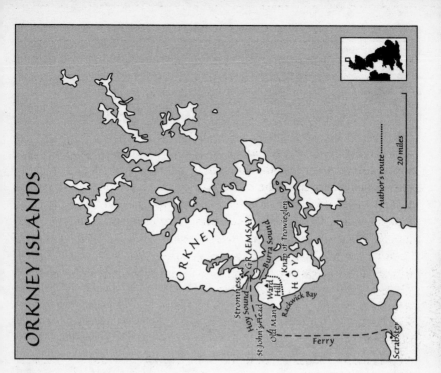

ORKNEY ISLANDS

ORKNEY

GRAEMSAY

Burra Sound

Knap of Trowieglen

Stromness

Hoy Sound

HOY

St John's Head

Ward Hill

Old Man

Rackwick Bay

Ferry

Scrabster

Author's route ....

20 miles

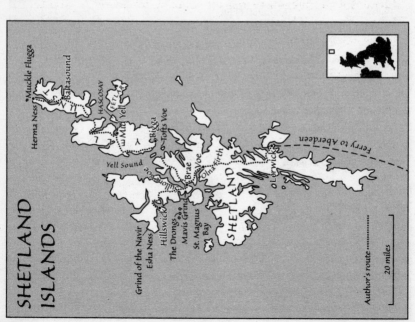

SHETLAND ISLANDS

Muckle Flugga

Herma Ness

Baltasound

N

UNST

HASCOSAY

FETLAR

Mid Yell

Brough

Yell Sound

YELL

Gluss

Tofts Voe

Sullom Voe

Grind of the Navir

Esha Ness

Hillswick

The Drongs

Mavis Grind

St Magnus Bay

Brae

Voe

Olna Firth

Lerwick

SHETLAND

Ferry to Aberdeen

Author's route ....

20 miles

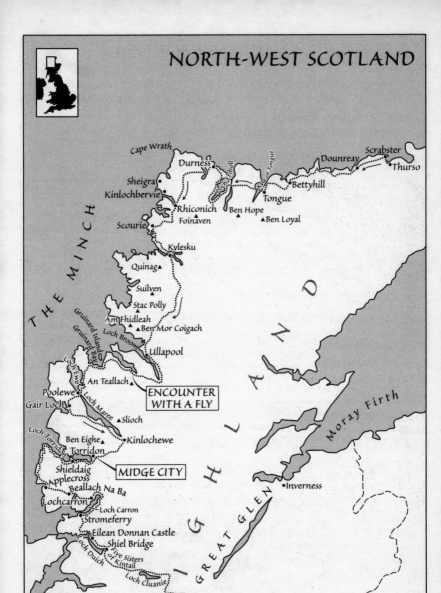

NORTH-WEST SCOTLAND

Cape Wrath

Durness

Scrabster

Dounreay

Thurso

Sheigra

Bettyhill

Kinlochbervie

Tongue

Rhiconich

Ben Hope

Ben Loyal

Foinaven

Scourie

Kylesku

Quinag

THE MINCH

Suilven

Stac Polly

Am Fhidleah

Loch Broom

Ben Mor Coigach

Gruinard Island

Gruinard Bay

Ullapool

Loch Ewe

An Teallach

ENCOUNTER WITH A FLY

Poolewe

Gair Loch

Loch Maree

Slioch

HIGHLAND

Moray Firth

Loch Torridon

Ben Eighe

Kinlochewe

Torridon

MIDGE CITY

Shieldaig

Applecross

Beallach Na Ba

Inverness

Lochcarron

Loch Carron

Stromeferry

GREAT GLEN

Eilean Donnan Castle

Shiel Bridge

Loch Duich

Five Sisters of Kintail

Loch Cluanie

Invergarry

Author's route ············

25 miles

THE HIGHLANDS AND BORDER

HIGHLAND

GRAMPIAN

Spean Bridge

▲ Ben Nevis
Fort William

Glen Coe

Author's route ··············

25 miles

TAYSIDE

Oban

Dundee

Loch Fyne

CENTRAL

Stirling

FIFE

Lochgilphead

STRATH

NEAR DEATH
EXPERIENCE
AT 666 MILES

Glasgow

Edinburgh

LOTHIAN

Cleonaig

Lochranza

Ardrossan

CLYDE

BORDERS

ARRAN

Kilmarnock

Brodick   ferry

Firth of Clyde

Cumnock

ENCOUNTER
WITH A LEECH

Mull of Kintyre

Carronbridge

DUMFRIES & GALLOWAY

Dumfries

Gretna
Green

Annan

Solway Firth

CUMBRIA

Sound of Jura

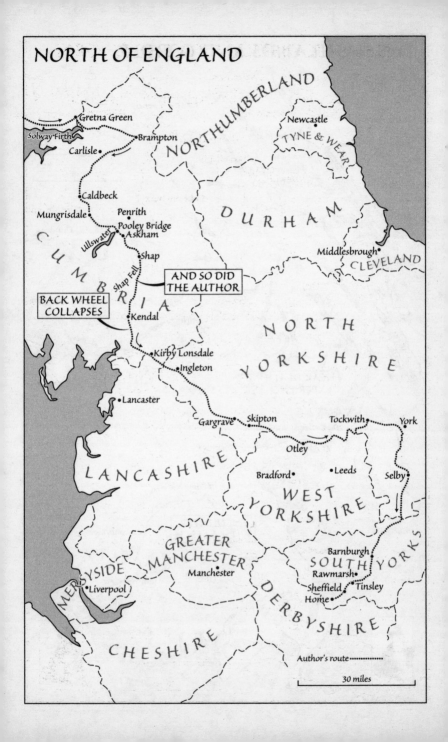

NORTH OF ENGLAND

Gretna Green
Solway Firth
Brampton
Carlisle
NORTHUMBERLAND
Newcastle
TYNE & WEAR
Caldbeck
Mungrisdale
Penrith
Pooley Bridge
Ullswater
Askham
DURHAM
Middlesbrough
CLEVELAND
Shap
AND SO DID THE AUTHOR
Shap Fell
BACK WHEEL COLLAPSES
CUMBRIA
Kendal
NORTH
Kirby Lonsdale
Ingleton
YORKSHIRE
Lancaster
Gargrave
Skipton
Tockwith
York
Otley
LANCASHIRE
Bradford
Leeds
Selby
WEST
YORKSHIRE
GREATER
MANCHESTER
Manchester
MERSEYSIDE
Liverpool
Barnburgh
SOUTH YORKS
Rawmarsh
Sheffield
Tinsley
Home
DERBYSHIRE
CHESHIRE
Author's route ....
30 miles

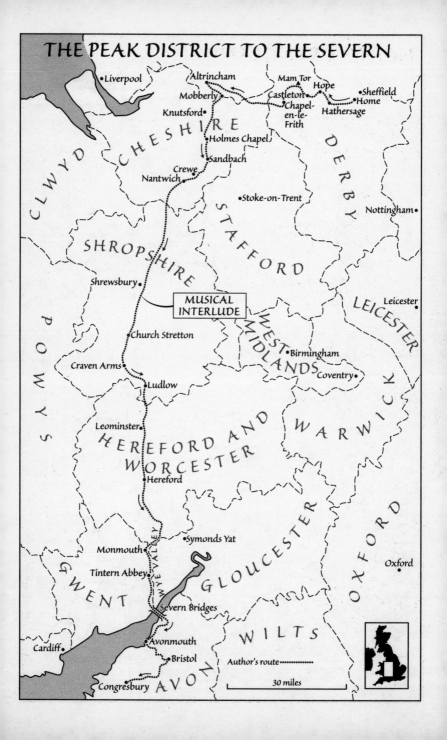

THE PEAK DISTRICT TO THE SEVERN

Liverpool

Altrincham • Mam Tor • Hope • Sheffield
Mobberly • Castleton • Home
Knutsford • Chapel-en-le-Frith • Hathersage

CLWYD

CHESHIRE

DERBY

Holmes Chapel

Sandbach

Crewe
Nantwich

Stoke-on-Trent

Nottingham •

SHROPSHIRE

STAFFORD

LEICESTER

Shrewsbury

Leicester •

MUSICAL
INTERLUDE

WEST
MIDLANDS

Church Stretton

Birmingham

Craven Arms

Coventry •

Ludlow

WARWICK

Leominster

HEREFORD AND
WORCESTER

Hereford

POWYS

Monmouth • Symonds Yat

GWENT

Tintern Abbey •

OXFORD

Oxford •

GLOUCESTER

WYE VALLEY

Severn Bridges

Cardiff •

Avonmouth

Bristol

WILTS

AVON

Author's route ••••••••••

Congresbury

30 miles

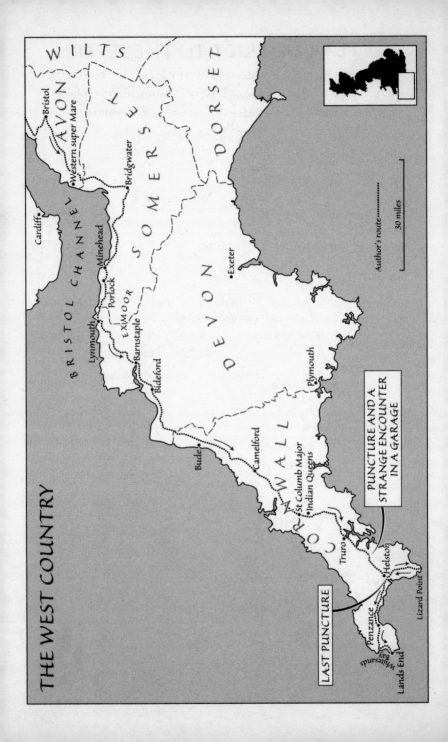

THE WEST COUNTRY

WILTS

AVON
Bristol
Weston super Mare

Cardiff

BRISTOL CHANNEL

Minehead
Portlock
EXMOOR
Lynmouth
Barnstaple
Bideford

SOMERSET
Bridgwater

DORSET

DEVON
Exeter

Plymouth

Bude

CORNWALL
Camelford
St Columb Major
Indian Queens

PUNCTURE AND A
STRANGE ENCOUNTER
IN A GARAGE

LAST PUNCTURE

Truro
Helston
Penzance
Whitesands Bay
Lands End
Lizard Point

Author's route

30 miles

During the journey described in these pages I was constantly asked the same five questions. Here, for those who can't be bothered to read the book, are the answers. The questions can be found at the back.

a. No

b. No

c. 30–40

d. None

e. Oh, fuck off

THE BEAST

1

Pilgrims, Plans and Pains

As dawn broke on the morning of 23rd April 1997, Chris Bonington's British Sepu Kangri expedition was camped on the Tibetan Plateau outside Nakchu, one of the coldest, highest and certainly ugliest cities in Tibet. I was there as expedition film-maker. All of us were numb with cold and suffering in varying degrees from the sudden gain in altitude, for we had driven here from Lhasa in a day. We tottered around, trying to adjust to the blinding sunlight reflecting off a smattering of new snow. The dirt road stretched away to the north. Suddenly John Porter and I noticed a strange movement, not a tractor or a yak or a bicycle. As it grew larger, we realised with a kind of shocked fascination that it was a man, a pilgrim, prostrating his length in the road, as he inched his way south towards the holy city of Lhasa, still well over a hundred miles away. He appeared to have no baggage and was wearing only his traditional Tibetan clothing. He was on his own. How had he survived the cruel night temperatures? Oblivious to our presence, he moved slowly past. We were awestruck. Where had he come from? How long would it take him to get to Lhasa? I just hoped his faith in Buddhism was justified – it seemed a pretty gruelling thing to do if it was all wasted effort.

But, though I'm no Buddhist, nor anything else for that matter, I could appreciate the rigour and dedication of this man's self-imposed act of faith and even see how he might get the same sort of high as the long-distance runner. For days after we had gone our separate ways I thought about him and wondered how far he had travelled. A month later, on our return from the mountain, we looked out for him at roughly the distance we guessed he might have covered as we approached Lhasa, but to no avail.

Later, on 29th April 2000, the vivid memory of that lone pilgrim came back to me as I pedalled an appallingly overloaded bicycle out of the port of Lerwick in the Shetland Islands. Unlike the pilgrim, who presumably was sustained by his inner belief in the Wheel of Life, I had to rely mainly on the inner tubes and wheels of my bike. Unlike him, I was not making this journey as an expression of faith. In fact, as I left Lerwick and started the gruelling grind up the first big hill, I didn't really know why I had set myself the task of cycling from the northernmost tip of Britain to the opposite end of the mainland. I just hoped that somewhere along the way I might find out.

It would be an understatement to say that 1999 had not been a happy year. A relationship on which I had, perhaps unrealistically, placed high expectation came to an end and, as a distraction, I threw myself into a commission I had been given to write the biography of Chris Bonington. But writing is a lonely activity with too much time for soul-searching. To cope with my burgeoning weight, caused by comfort-eating and drinking, I joined Body and Soul, a gym at the local YMCA. In the company of fellow author Joe Simpson, also struggling with an unwritten book, I grunted and sweated the months away. We also frequented the Edge, a state-of-the-art climbing wall only a few minutes from my house in Nether Edge, Sheffield. To add to my woes, I developed tennis elbow and a right kneecap that threatened to whiz across the gym like an errant frisbee unless restrained by an ever-increasing swathe of elastic bandages. I was forced to give up all but the gentlest exercises in the gym, and rock-climbing was out of the question. I began to really feel my age. Riddled with depression, loneliness and self-doubt, I was on a downward spiral, and only the support of close friends like *High* magazine editor Geoff Birtles and my daughters Gemma and Becky kept me together.

When, to my relief, the biography was published in October 1999 and the documentary I had helped make of Chris Bonington's two Sepu Kangri expeditions was also finished, I felt I had to try to draw a line under the past twelve months. Easier said than done, for the question, what next? began to intrude. There was no way I was going to get involved in another expedition, despite everyone I knew telling me I would soon change my mind. Since I first went to the Trango Tower in 1976, I had been to the Himalaya, either filming or climbing, or both, fifteen times, as well as on several expeditions to the Andes and Caucasus and on three to Africa. I began to feel trapped like a long-term heroin addict in a way of life that had almost ceased to give any pleasure, but seemed nearly impossible to give up. I could still get a brief high in the adrenalin rush of a new project, organising a film, dealing with sponsors, meeting new people and enjoying the spurious trappings of Andy Warhol's fifteen minutes of fame. But now this was not enough.

There was also another nagging doubt. Since the disastrous summer of 1986 when I had been on K2 when thirteen men and women died, including British climbers Julie Tullis and one of my closest friends, Al Rouse, I wasn't only losing interest in expeditions, I was seriously questioning my own attitude to making documentaries about them. The relentless media dumbing down of an activity I loved was exacerbated by the thought that my own contribution through films and books might actually be a part of the same process. I had always (rather naively) thought that my film ideas were at least motivated by a desire to communicate the reality of mountaineering without relying on superlatives, exaggerated claims and false heroics. Now I wasn't so sure.

As the millennium approached, I began to think about some sort of low-key solo journey. I had done more than my fair share of what Joe Simpson once called 'credit card adventures' and felt increasingly that travel to virtually anywhere in the world is now so easy that it is self-delusion for us climbers to kid ourselves that somehow we alone are not tourists. On Sepu Kangri with Chris Bonington I had been immensely privileged to visit those remote mountains of Eastern Tibet, just as I had been back in 1981 on the Mount Kongur expedition to the Sinkiang province of China. But Chris had already done the real exploration in the years before the main expeditions. Uncertainty and danger were both easily available, but I had to admit that I had probably shot my bolt in these directions. I have always been a moderate but competent performer; very occasionally surprising myself with ascents of rock-climbs I thought beyond my abilities. But since 1986 I had grown increasingly frightened of anything remotely serious and, to my consternation, a bi-product of the K2 trauma was homesickness and insecurity. The thrill of the unknown I had once craved had been sated. Before flying to Tibet in 1998, I had joked that I had started feeling homesick at least a week before leaving Sheffield. Except it wasn't a joke.

So, having almost justified spending the rest of my days gardening, taking up bowls and visiting DIY centres, I was surprised when I found myself, a propos of nothing, thinking about a bicycle ride. It would have to be solo, unsupported, and a reasonably long way. I was not remotely interested in the Land's End to John O'Groats ride with all its undertones of competition and charitable fund-raising. I wanted something much more open-ended with different elements involved, like walking and climbing, as well as cycling. In my youth I had done a fair amount of cycling around the Home Counties and had once cycled from Ealing to Land's End and back with school friends. But a subsequent biking holiday in North Wales coincided with the beginning of my climbing career and the bike was abandoned almost overnight.

Then about seven years ago the poet, climber and lecturer Terry Gifford and I decided to climb Fionn Buttress on Carnmore

Crag in one of the more remote areas of north-west Scotland. Terry suggested using mountain bikes to cut down on the long walk in, and for the first time in years I rediscovered the joys of pedalling. Even better was the freewheeling on the way back. This was the life. Shortly afterwards I bought a decent mountain bike for myself and decided its maiden ride should be out to a favourite pub, the Moon in Stoney Middleton, to have Sunday lunch with my oldest and best friend, climbing guru Paul Nunn. Cycling out of Sheffield, I overtook one of those elderly joggers who clearly ought not to be doing it at all. Purple-faced, with one foot only just overlapping the other, he tottered towards the inevitable heart attack. I swept past him and soon found myself clicking down the gears as I hit the first big hill. Soon my legs were just a blur as I pedalled furiously in the lowest possible gear. Then, to my horror, I heard the dread shuffle of ancient flapping training shoes behind me. The old fart even had the cheek to wish me good morning and plodded past me up towards the Foxhouse Inn. Later I did overtake him, but it didn't really count as by then I was free-wheeling almost out of control at what seemed like 80 miles an hour down Froggatt Hill. After two or three pints Paul took pity on me and put the bike in his car for the ride back to Sheffield. Despite this inauspicious start, and without getting too fanatical, I actually began going out regularly. But when the bike was stolen out of my garden shed I kept thinking about replacing it but never did.

Now the idea of another bike was edging into my frontal lobes I had to consider where I would ride the thing. An early decision was a visit to the Shetland Islands. I had been to the Orkneys three times already, climbing the Old Man of Hoy in 1983, and filming on it in 1994 and '97. I have also climbed in the Outer Hebrides and St Kilda and, though I knew there wasn't a lot of climbing on Shetland, its very remoteness was the big attraction.

Slowly I evolved a plan – to cycle from the furthest point north in Shetland, through to the Orkneys, around the north and west coasts of Scotland, down to the Lake District, then through the Yorkshire Dales to finish at home base in Sheffield. But why stop there? The itinerary soon became extended to Bristol, where I used to work, the West Country and Land's End. In my original dreams I would try and do a climb or two that I had never done before on various crags and mountains en route, whilst meeting up with old friends along the way, who would provide company or hospitality or, better still, both.

Two things were absolutely clear to me from the word go. There was to be no element of competition or endurance involved; and no time limit on how long it would take to complete. Secondly, I was not going to complicate the ride by doing it for charity. This was not because I don't approve of these ventures, far from it – I had undertaken a climbing marathon for charity back in 1983 when a friend and I did one hundred climbs in ten days. This time, I thought, I would be lucky to do ten climbs in a hundred days (and I was quite right). Though I flirted with the idea for a while, I didn't pursue making a film either, where I would inevitably end up at the beck and call of a TV crew. This would be a journey for myself on entirely my own terms.

In the past I had become all too familiar with baffled incomprehension from friends and family as I tried to justify yet another departure to a mountain somewhere in India, Tibet or South America. But this time, to my surprise, everyone was incredibly enthusiastic, though I had a dark suspicion that this could be simply relief from having to put up with my gloomy presence for a couple of months. Frequently I was told it was a brilliant idea and how lucky I was to be able to indulge it. Strangely enough, this time, the only person to be unconvinced was myself. What was I letting myself in for?

The sun was shining, my hangover was almost bearable, it was 1st January and I had exactly four months to transform myself into an athlete, albeit a geriatric one. I told myself I had better get out into Derbyshire and walk up a hill. Which is what I did. So, it appeared, had the entire population of Sheffield, for it was a stunning winter's day with a cloud inversion covering the Derwent Valley. Kodak's profits were soaring and White Edge, the ridge above Froggatt and Curbar Edges was just about gridlocked. Fearing cheery encounters with hearty outdoor folk with no hangovers and rosy cheeks, I plunged down Froggatt Hill into the cold mist and drove to a car park on the A6. I walked up Brushfield Hough to Priestcliffe and Taddington, then around to Dimin Dale and Deep Dale and back to the car. It was only about five miles but it was a start, of sorts.

I am, always have been, and always will be, deeply lazy. 'Never put off till tomorrow what can be put off until next week' has been my motto. (It has taken me almost all day to get round to writing this sentence, despite promising myself a 9 a.m. start.) Consequently, preparations for my 'little outing', as I began to think of it, were desultory, to say the least. I had a shrewd suspicion that training by actually riding a bicycle would be so soul-destroying that I would almost certainly talk myself out of ever starting. Instead I continued a series of winter walks in Derbyshire. These were normally solitary but occasionally in the company of my friends, collectively known as the Old Spice Girls – Pams I and II, Hilary and Rita. We squelched our way round boggy farmyards or boulder-hopped through Chee Dale, avoiding immersion in the swollen waters of the River Wye. I don't think these walks did a great deal for my physical well-being but, especially when I was on my own, I could get into the state of mind I thought might be useful in coping with a long journey – not exactly in a trance, but not far off it.

As the weeks rolled by and time speeded up, I worried about the practicalities of the project. To be truthful, only one part of me worried; the other kept saying relax, it's no big deal, you're only riding a bike – you could start tomorrow if you had to. Before my last two trips to Tibet there had been endless planning and frequent meetings to get the TV documentary off the ground, then at the very last minute slinging a few clothes and bits of gear in a rucksack. The second trip hardly involved that, for I had never properly unpacked from the first. But the ride was new territory for me. What could I reasonably carry? What did I really need? I had bought a tiny one-man tent at a knock-down price from Terra Nova, who had loaned all the tents for both the Sepu Kangri expeditions. One cold March day I drove out into Derbyshire and found a secluded lay-by and put it up on a patch of grass. I was unimpressed. It really was very small indeed. With only a single hoop tensioned by half a dozen guy ropes, it seemed incredibly fragile. Lying in it was depressing and claustrophobic, with my nose only inches away from the flapping inner skin. Could I really put up with living like this for a couple of months? I took it down and tried to forget about it.

What about clothes and climbing gear? I was due to start at the end of April and knew that northern Scotland could still be very cold. The Shetlands would be windy as well. Cycling was almost all hard aerobic work. Even my little forays out of Sheffield had been achieved only by sweating like a bull. Freewheeling downhill, on the other hand, was a quick way to lose body heat.

The clothes problem was solved thanks to the generosity of Sue Reay at Berghaus, who had supplied a vast amount of kit over the years in exchange for exposure in TV documentaries. This time Sue did it, I imagine, out of sheer kindness, for a portly fifty-seven-year-old was hardly likely to be a potential fashion model for the Berghaus catalogue.

As for climbing gear, I decided to ride in a pair of lightweight walking boots and take only a pair of rock shoes, a harness and chalk bag, plus a couple of walking poles to ease the pain in my knees. I assumed that if I climbed with anyone else they would supply ropes and a rack of gear and if I were on my own I would be soloing anyway, so I would only need the shoes.

As you can tell, I was horribly ignorant of all the little bits and pieces of knowledge that I had come to take for granted on expeditions. But I was too proud/lazy to ask anyone for advice and it was only at a chance meeting with an old friend from North Wales that I received any practical tips. Terry Hetherley is slightly older and fatter than I am and I met him by chance in a Sheffield pub. He had done the John O'Groats to Land's End ride a couple of years before. His advice was succinct and brutally honest. First, remember that nearly all cycling is uphill. Second, the wind is always against you. Third, don't camp; stay in bed and breakfast. Fourth, don't expect it ever to get easier. Fifth, don't imagine you will lose weight. I took all his points with a pinch of salt but the first two did make some sort of sense. Not much of Britain, particularly on the western side, is flat. Going downhill is quicker than uphill, therefore, most of your time is spent pushing the pedals and fighting gravity. The second point is also true, especially if you are doing the ride north to south, for you are also travelling mainly east to west, against the prevailing wind. But even in flat calm you will have the illusion that you are cycling against the wind as you pick up speed. Only on those rare occasions with a strong following wind do you feel that God has given you a break. Even then you quickly take it for granted.

As March came and went my friends questioned me with increasing frequency about when I would be acquiring that basic piece of equipment, the bicycle. It was obvious that the old mountain bike I had bought off Geoff Birtles the previous autumn was inadequate. For a while I had high hopes of a freebie from Raleigh Bicycles. I had written a letter to their PR Department that was, I thought, a minor masterpiece in the art of begging. In it I pointed out the good publicity they would get by sponsoring me. The access I had built up over the years to the media through films, books, articles and lectures would guarantee a lot of exposure. It was an offer they simply couldn't refuse. I never even got a reply. I consoled myself with the thought that at least I could give them a bit of bad publicity (here it is), but the ominous realisation grew that I would actually have to spend good money on a bike. In the forlorn hope of a reply from Raleigh I put off the evil day until the last possible moment. Then, in the company of my old friend Mike Richardson who now lives with my second ex-wife Laraine, and has thus become my common-law husband, I made the fateful trip to W. E. James Cycles, the best cycle shop in Sheffield.

I am not a gear freak. As far as rock-climbing and mountaineering go, I have never lusted over equipment catalogues or spent hours in climbing shops discussing the pros and cons of karabiner design or the style of rock shoes. I also loathe shopping in general. So the trip to the bike shop was not going to be fun. I hoped by taking Mike along, as both adviser and interpreter, I could simply sign a cheque for God only knows how much and go home again.

As I'd feared, the conversation with the assistant quickly degenerated into techno-babble and I gazed blankly at a mass of chromium wheels and aluminium frames enlivened with stripes, chequers and illegible lettering. They were also decorated with mind-boggling fluorescent price tags. I only wanted a push bike for Christ's sake – I could have bought a decent second-hand Jag for less than the asking price of some of these top-of-the-range models. Eventually we settled on a hybrid – neither fish nor fowl, a cross between a mountain bike and a road bike. It was strong and solid but not so heavy and chunky that riding on a road would be a misery. It would have to bear a huge weight – me, plus two rear-wheel panniers and a handlebar attachment in which I would carry everyday essentials like maps, money and cameras. The deciding factor was not actually based on design or suitability but on a magic trade mark emblazoned on the aluminium frame: Claude Butler. Though I knew full well that it was now only a trade mark, my mind went spinning back to my early teens when Claude Butler had the same sort of iconic status in my mind as Ferrari cars, Slazenger cricket bats, Elvis Presley 78s, Passing

Cloud cigarettes and Hawker Hunter jet fighters. Shuddering at the price, plus all the extra accessories deemed essential, I left the shop with not much change from six hundred pounds, and with no bike either, which wouldn't actually be ready and roadworthy for another week. This left only a few days before I was due to set off on Friday 28th April, so any further training was clearly out of the question, which pleased me.

As on every expedition I have ever been involved with, I was rapidly entering ground rush mode. The number of things to do multiplied as the time to do them in divided. What had begun four months earlier with mild excitement and anticipation was fast descending into dread and fright. Why was I doing this? Could I even at this late stage chicken out? The answer was no, especially once Jackie Birtles won the pub quiz jackpot, and the Old Spice Girls decided to put all Jackie's winnings towards a farewell meal the night before I left.

By Thursday afternoon I had at last packed up most of my kit and attached the panniers to the bike. I was also taking a rucksack strapped on top of the panniers which I hadn't packed yet. Even so, I was aghast at the total weight and pedalled gingerly up my road on a short ride round the perimeter of Nether Edge Hospital. It was only just uphill but I quickly resorted to the lowest gear and my legs spun round while the world almost stood still. Eventually I turned right and right again and the bike lurched off almost out of control back down to my house. At least, I thought, it is downhill to Sheffield Midland station, and the first chunk of the ride in the Shetlands should be reasonably flat.

LEAVING THE GRANITE CITY

2

Trains and Boats and Chains

I woke at six with that awful thud of alarm that you get when you remember that something grim is about to happen. Monday mornings, having failed to do my maths homework, was an early example, followed (in more or less chronological order) by exams, important cricket matches, early starts on Alpine climbs, getting married and leaving on expeditions from Heathrow. I had a self-inflicted headache and unsurprisingly the packing hadn't done itself during the night. I had pre-booked tickets on the trains to Aberdeen and the ferry to Lerwick. The Sheffield train left at 9.30 but even so I gave myself a whole hour to get there. As I wheeled the bike outside, David, my next-door neighbour took a couple of photographs for me on my camera. Then I set the burglar alarm, locked up and hoisted myself carefully onto the saddle, wincing at a sharp pain in my ribs, acquired a few days before while twisting to pick up some gear and sneezing violently.

As I could freewheel quite a lot of the way to the station I couldn't tell just how heavy the fully loaded bike was. But when I got there I found out instantly, because I had to cart it over a bridge to the right platform. It took every ounce of strength to hump it up the stairs and I nearly let it go on the way down. The first stage was to York, then change trains in Edinburgh, then on to Aberdeen. The York train was a run-down two-carriage affair that made a noise like an old bus, and travelled about as fast, out through the grim Don Valley, past the shopping centre I always called Meadow Hell, then on through Rotherham and Mexborough. Gazing out at the scene of industrial wasteland I consoled myself with the thought that my return would be via the altogether more inspiring Peak District, by Stanage Edge and down my favourite Ringinglow Road approach to home, with perhaps a drink at the Norfolk Arms before a triumphant entry into Sheffield. Hang on, what am I thinking about? Don't indulge in fantasies, Curran. Concentrate on the present.

I manhandled the bike off the train at York station to a scene of almost surreal bedlam. A mass of kilted youths wearing bright orange curly-haired wigs were shouting and chanting as policemen in lemon yellow jackets tried to keep order. What seemed like a whole football crowd was trying to board the Edinburgh train and I remembered with sinking heart that for the first time the Rugby League Cup Final was to be played at Murrayfield instead of Wembley. What's more, the finalists were the Bradford Bulls and the Leeds Rhinos, and supporters of both sides were being herded onto the same train.

The guards van was at one end of the train and my pre-booked ticket was for a seat in Carriage A, at the other. I cursed the bloke in the ticket office, who must have known that I would be separated from my bike and worldly goods by twelve carriages – the only non-rugby league supporter going to Edinburgh. What's more, when I finally got to my seat, I realised that the same stupid bastard had put me in the only smoking compartment on the whole train. As soon as I sat down the woman sitting next to me lit up. I coughed absentmindedly and a screeching pain shot through my ribs. God Almighty, was I going to have to hold my breath all the way to Edinburgh? On the other side of the aisle sat four rather buxom young ladies cracking open can after can of Heineken Special Brew and blowing smoke in each other's faces. Their conversation was mainly quick-fire repartee at the expense of anyone and everyone, particularly male supporters of the opposition. Some of it was imaginative and hilarious – all of it unprintable. Please don't make me laugh, I prayed through the haze of tobacco smoke.

To my surprise, both sets of supporters retained their good humour all the way to Edinburgh, even sharing each other's drinks and ciggies. The policemen travelling on the train had an easy job and I wondered why it was that the supporters of virtually every sport bar football could travel in this way. Put any two sets of Premier Division fans together and you would end up with mayhem at the very least and quite possibly serious injury or death. The worst that happened on this journey was a heated discussion over some obtuse interpretations of the laws of the game that I couldn't understand. Both sides of the argument were put forward by Leeds supporters and when voices became slightly raised they were quickly restrained by both sets of fans. I was impressed.

We arrived at Edinburgh Waverley station almost forty-five minutes late, which left me only ten minutes to catch the Aberdeen train. First I had to fight my way against the mass of passengers jostling towards the exit to pick the bike up at the far end of the train. Then I found that the platform for Aberdeen was miles away over a bridge in a remote corner of the station. This time there was a lift on the bridge, which made life a bit easier, but time was ticking away and I feared that if I missed the train I might also miss the ferry, which only ran every three or four days to the Shetlands. I pushed the bike as fast as I could walk before suddenly remembering I could actually get on it and ride, which I did, catching the train with only seconds to spare.

The carriages were brand new and even had a trendy bicycle storage rack painted in a pastel blue. We glided out of Waverley station towards the Forth Bridge. I gazed at flooded fields, the result of recent heavy gales, and remembered seeing Murrayfield on the TV news the night before, with officials knee deep in water trying to get the pitch playable. Now it was a beautiful spring day with the sun reflected off the floods, then suddenly, strobe-like, off the waters of the Forth, as the train clattered over the famous old bridge and shadows of the massive rusty structure alternated in quick succession with beams of slanting light.

Opposite me sat a most peculiar couple, sad relics of the punk era, liberally festooned with safety pins and studs inserted into every visible orifice. Both were small and very round, both had violently dyed orange hair (the colour of many of my travelling companions that day). Both spoke in such broad Glaswegian accents as to be virtually unintelligible to my uneducated Sassenach ears. This was compounded by the not too difficult deduction that they had enjoyed a long and liquid lunch. But what really puzzled me was the fact that, whereas the smaller and rounder of the two was almost certainly female, the sex of the other was not at all obvious. It was a situation that he (or she) seemed to relish as my bewilderment grew. To my embarrassment he/she bombarded me with questions about my journey. He or she found my answers and my accent hysterically funny, and translated everything I said for the benefit of his/her companion/ lover/wife/sister. She spent her time gazing adoringly at her husband/brother/sister/friend and saying very little. Eventually they got off at Perth, clutching a mass of strangely shaped parcels that I hoped for their sakes they had purchased before lunch, and I was free to gaze out of the window once more.

At Aberdeen I pedalled cautiously out of the station car park and into a one-way system that seemed to lead exactly in the wrong direction. So I got off and pushed and after only a couple of minutes found myself freewheeling down a greasy ramp into the bowels of the Lerwick ferry, meeting as I did so that familiar car-ferry smell of diesel, oil, salt water, sick, stale chip fat and beer, combined with the faint grey haze left by the smoke of several million cigarettes.

There was hardly a soul on board and those that were had gathered inevitably in the bar. As the engines rumbled most of us drifted to the stern to stare at the impressive panorama of the Granite City as it slid away. In the twilight a father and son stood at the very end of the breakwater, which was painted a dull orange. It reminded me of a piece of 1960s sculpture, but I couldn't think which. They waved at nobody in particular, so I waved back, faintly embarrassed. Then they were swallowed up in the dusk and became part of the dense grey block of land that soon merged with the sea and sky. It was a calm evening, which was welcome, for I am a useless sailor and it is a twelve-hour voyage to Lerwick.

The deserted lounge was stiflingly hot and in the corner a big colour TV played quietly to itself. I had braved the restaurant and had the first of many plates of Scottish chips, this one decorated with a couple of horrible sausages and a congealed egg. I washed it down with a pint of lager, then watched the 9 p.m. news before tipping up the arm rests, stretching out across three seats and trying to go to sleep without coughing. It was not a dreamless oblivion, but I didn't expect it would be. As it grew light I abandoned any further pretence of sleep and stared out at a misty dawn. When the ship had docked, faint grey shapes of what I took to be Lerwick began to form and by the time I had gone to the car deck and retrieved the bike the bow doors were open. A couple of container lorries thundered away, followed by a handful of cars, followed by me. I had set wheels in the Shetlands.

Here are a few facts that I for one didn't know before I set out. Muckle Flugga Lighthouse is just over 150 miles north of Dunnet Head, the most northerly point on the Scottish mainland (not John O'Groats, which is the most north-easterly). The Shetlands are nearer the Arctic Circle than London, as close to Bergen in Norway as to Aberdeen and as far north as Anchorage in Alaska. Believe it or not, Muckle Flugga Lighthouse is further north than Cape Farewell, the southernmost tip of Greenland. There are more than one hundred islands, excluding innumerable sea stacks many of which have been climbed by that intrepid mountaineer and tax inspector, Mick Fowler. Only seventeen are inhabited. In the week I had available I would be able visit only three, which was barely scratching the surface.

First things first, I needed some breakfast and I cycled the mile or so from the grim grey docks to the old centre of Lerwick. So far so good. I found a tiny café and realised quickly that once again I had a language problem. Nobody seemed to find it difficult to understand me, but I found the soft Norwegian-sounding lilt hard to pick up. I went to the Tourist Office (the first of many such visits in the next months), bought a decent map and picked up a couple of handouts about campsites and bicycle touring. The former was short and to the point. There weren't any to speak of outside Lerwick and camping was normally at the discretion of the farmer or landowner. The bit about cycling wasn't exactly encouraging either, pointing out that the Shetlands were very windy, which I knew, and hilly, which I didn't. It advised cyclists to work on a much lower than average speed than they might have assumed and suggested 5–7 miles an hour was realistic. I prepared to scoff, imagining that this was written for the benefit of some totally unfit, possibly elderly, inexperienced first-time cyclist. Then I remembered I was one.

After a bit more pottering about and fiddling with various straps and buckles I couldn't put off the moment any longer and, at about the crack of midday, I pedalled solemnly out of Lerwick heading north. The second prophecy in the handout was fulfilled within minutes as the road took the first hill head on. I hadn't thought much about the possibility of getting off and pushing. In my mind I had imagined a gaunt bronzed figure, face contorted with effort, standing up on the pedals, while admiring pedestrians and passing motorists marvelled at the sight, possibly even applauding. In fact after about half a minute in the lowest gear (known to the cycling fraternity rather offensively, I felt, as the granny ring), I was going so slowly that I almost fell off. So I had to get off and push. The bike, like its owner, was apallingly, outrageously, mind-bogglingly heavy. Surely I didn't need to carry all this junk around for the next two months? At the rate I was plodding up the hill it would be more like two years before I got to Cornwall. The road curved round to the left and I looked back for a last glimpse of the berthed car ferry. I could so easily just freewheel back and get on it and scrap the whole daft idea. No sooner had the temptation crossed my mind than the horrible realization came that I simply couldn't give in, now or ever. I've started so I'll finish. The memory of that lone figure on the Tibetan Plateau returned. I amused myself with the thought that if, on the day he set off to Lhasa from his home, he had gone a hundred yards prostrating himself and then said, 'Oh bugger it' (or the Tibetan equivalent), and walked back to watch the Chinese equivalent of *Richard and Judy*, he would be remembered for years as the laughing stock of his village. There was no choice.

Eventually the road levelled out and after a couple of enjoyable minutes on the flat I plunged down an equally long hill almost all the way back to sea level – fun, but I could see that on the opposite side of a large sea loch a similar hill awaited. As I started the first bout of serious pedalling and gear changing, the chain flew off. Disconcerted, I saw that the gear mechanism seemed to have been knocked out of alignment at some stage of the journey. I bent it straight but soon realised that something was wrong with the cable tension and the bloody thing would jump a gear for no apparent reason. After a few miles I stopped and unpacked my brand new tool kit. It had cost a small fortune but I had very little idea what half the gadgets were for. Despite having almost no mechanical sense at all, I did spend a fair chunk of my teenage years tinkering with bikes, and hoped that miraculously my memory would serve me well. In fact, more by luck than good judgement, I managed to get the tensions right. After a drink and some chocolate I set off again, feeling rather pleased with myself. I would have felt less so had I realised that I'd left the tool kit by the side of the road, never to be seen again. A gentle breeze blew from the north but a wan sun made an appearance. Soon I found to my surprise that I was enjoying myself. Well, Curran, I thought, you're on your way.

The scenery was bleakly impressive, if not quite breathtaking.

The moorlands reminded me of the Peak District, peaty wastes, gently angled slopes, supporting only heather and bog, falling to a rocky coastline. Here, on the eastern shoreline, there were no cliffs to speak of, just boulders and shingle-strewn beaches bordering Dales Voe. 'Voe' is the name given to the sea lochs that penetrate all three main Shetland Islands. Sullom Voe is the best known, the site of the North Sea oil terminal, but virtually the whole coastline is made up of voes – Dales Voe, Wadbister Voe, Vidlin Voe, Orca Voe . . .

If the long views had a certain grandeur and simplicity of form, the close-ups were not so good. Since Lerwick I appeared to have been following the trail of an endless drunken travelling riot. Dozens of empty half bottles of whisky, thousands of beer cans and frequent wrecks of cars littered the verges. Conservation seemed to be an alien concept. I remembered one climbing trip to the Hebrides being similarly amazed, driving up to the Butt of Lewis, at the number of abandoned cars. Many of them had boulders placed thoughtfully on their bonnets to stop the panels scything off the heads of passers by when the hinges rusted through and the gales blew in off the Atlantic. I wondered why the profession of scrap merchant had failed to take hold up here. Presumably it just isn't economic to salvage the wrecks, which would have to be taken to the mainland for recycling.

Meanwhile, I pedalled from can to can, from bottle to bottle, trying to imagine the state of the occupants of the cars. Perhaps they all wore top hats and evening dress and carried balloons. Or were they Vikings with horns in their helmets? If they were, there wouldn't have been much rape and pillaging to do, for there just wasn't anyone or anything around, apart from the eponymous little ponies scattered around the landscape, who looked much too gentle and cuddly for anyone to do any harm to at all.

3

It's a Long Way to Muckle Flugga

As I rode, I started to think about what I was going to do in the next few days. Before I set out, I had made only the vaguest of plans (i.e. none). I had written a list of places and approximate dates on a small piece of paper, but only two or three were fixed. The rest of the time, I could do whatever I pleased. The ghosts of Shipton and Tilman, who famously planned their Himalayan explorations on the back of an envelope, would be proud of me.

The first fixed date was to catch the weekly ferry to Stromness in the Orkneys the following Friday morning. This meant getting back to Lerwick, or very near it, by Thursday evening to be on the safe side. It was now Saturday afternoon. I wanted to cycle out to the west coast to the Esha Ness Lighthouse and the strangely named Grind of the Navir, reputed to be where some of the best rock-climbing in the Shetlands was to be found. From there, I would cycle along Sullom Voe to catch the ferry for the island of Yell and the next one for Unst, and the ride up to Herma Ness. From there you can see Muckle Flugga Lighthouse perched near Out Stack and the Rumblings. Then I'd cycle back to Lerwick. Suddenly a week seemed to be rather a short time, but a fortnight would be far too long and, in any case, I had another one of my few fixed dates lined up on Orkney, next weekend.

By late afternoon I had reached the village of Brae, which had a filling station and, to my relief, a small general store. I made a

IT'S A LONG WAY TO MUCKLE FLUGGA

point of always carrying enough food and drink to last a day or two but quickly realised that, here in the Shetlands, water could be a problem and I bought a two-litre bottle of mineral water. I had ridden only about twenty-five miles, which was no big deal but I was determined in these early days not to get either bored or shattered. Even so, I had the first intimations of saddle soreness and, slightly worryingly, bad pins and needles in both hands. In fact my right hand seemed quite numb.

Ahead of me, the road to Esha Ness dropped downhill and swept along the shoreline of Sullom Voe on my right, and St Magnus Bay on my left. A minor curiosity is that here the Atlantic Ocean and North Sea are separated by only a narrow causeway, known as Mavis Grind, which sounded vaguely suggestive. I wondered who Mavis was (and what she did to earn her name). It was here that the Vikings are supposed to have hauled their long-boats overland on their way from Norway to Iceland, Greenland and next stop America. Maybe Mavis gave them a send-off to remember. In the corner of a disused quarry I decided to camp.

It was an unprepossessing place, litter-strewn and boggy and it took some time to find a flat area and clear it of bits of broken glass, presumably from another bottle party I'd missed out on. I was surprised, on this first night, how long it took to get organised but I was pleased to find that, on pitching the tent for only the second time, it quickly felt like home – if a ridiculously small one. In addition to whatever daily ingredients I had bought to cook on my one-burner gas stove, I had brought only one small saucepan, one mug, one knife, fork and spoon (though I seemed to remember Bill Tilman dispensing with a fork and spoon), a small bag of herbs and spices, a few tea bags and some powdered milk. Tonight I made spaghetti (cooked in fizzy mineral water) with plenty of garlic and Parmesan cheese, knowing it was most unlikely in the near future that I would have to worry about causing offence in the malodorous breath department. Then I started to read the first of three paperbacks I had brought with me until the light faded. At the end of April up here in the Shetlands it didn't get dark until well after ten and even then it was for only a few hours. I dropped off to sleep feeling quite pleased with myself and relieved that, as usual, once a trip was underway the awful pre-match nerves had disappeared. I wished the homesickness would as well.

I awoke to a faint pattering of rain on the tent and unzipped the flysheet to a dreary dawn. The cloud base was only a few metres above me and it was quite cold, but not too windy. A good night's sleep recharges the mental batteries and I suddenly realised that I could leave almost all my luggage hidden here and ride out and back to the Grind of the Navir with just my rock shoes, chalk bag, a camera and a bit of food. I would also take my repair kit I thought, rather impressed at my foresight. An hour later, and having strewn all my possessions far and wide, I admitted that I'd left the bloody thing by the roadside. I also realised that I hadn't even got a puncture repair outfit, though I had brought two spare inner tubes and a spare tyre. These, combined with the handles on the knife, fork and spoon to use as tyre levers, would have to do until I returned to Lerwick (assuming there was a bike shop there).

After hiding all my possessions around the boulder debris of the quarry and praying that nobody would find them, I set off. I would like to say I was delightfully unladen. Well, unladen I certainly was, but to my disappointment there didn't seem to be a great deal of difference as I once again failed on the first steep hill and had to get off and push. Over the next months I had several days riding unladen and it was always the same – imagining I would feel a supercharge of energy that never arrived. As I pedalled rather grimly uphill against the wind I hit the cloud base and while it wasn't actually raining, the mist quickly condensed and dripped down my helmet and jacket. My hands quickly went numb and once again my right hand seemed to be a lot worse than my left. After ten miles it did start raining and my enthusiasm for soloing even an easy climb on a remote and unknown sea cliff diminished. I rode past the turn-off to Esha Ness and, a mile or so further on, I arrived in the tiny village of Hillswick where the St Magnus Bay Hotel was open for coffee.

This was quite the biggest and most imposing building I had seen since Lerwick, a fine clapboard structure that looked as though it had been transplanted from the suburbs of New England. I was puzzled: wood seemed to be a curious material to choose on an island where trees are conspicuous by their absence. Maybe its construction had used up the last remnants?

I thawed out with a coffee, followed by another one. I listened to the conversations between a waitress and the landlady, finding that female voices are far easier to understand than male. A young woman arrived and told how she had helped in the delivery of two pairs of twins the night before. This seemed an amazing coincidence for such a tiny village until I realised she was talking about the lambing season which was in full swing.

I paid for the coffees and pottered around Hillswick for an hour or so, hoping the sun would break through or that I would suddenly have a fit of enthusiasm for frightening myself on a sea cliff. In the end, I rode back to the Esha Ness road and went a couple of miles uphill until a new panorama was revealed. Behind me a line of stubby sea stacks, like ancient teeth, marched across St Magnus Bay. They are called the Drongs. Ahead the road dipped and I could see, just below the cloud base, empty moorland leading to the coast. A dim yellow light far out at sea suggested that the weather might eventually improve but now it was drizzling steadily and my heart wasn't in it. I turned round and pedalled back to Mavis Grind feeling, shamefacedly, that I'd failed my first test. By now two fingers of my right hand seemed to be permanently numb. No amount of rubbing made any difference and I was puzzled. Could this just be caused by vibration? It didn't seem very likely – the handlebars were padded with rubber grips and I was wearing padded leather fingerless gloves. More pressing (literally), was that I had developed a very sore bottom.

I found my kit (undisturbed) and re-erected the tent. Even at this early stage I loved the moment when I could crawl in, unroll the sleeping bag, inflate the Thermorest and shut out the big wide world. With the stove on and water bubbling and my paperback to read I was perfectly happy. Conversely, packing up in the mornings never got any better. I did eventually develop a system of sorts, but I always hated the moment when the tent came down and I was temporarily homeless. Surrounded by overflowing panniers, still with bits and pieces of clothing and cooking gear all to be crammed in, I would feel lonely and vulnerable. Strangely though, the feeling wore off the moment I got on the bike and pedalled the first few yards. Suddenly I had regained control – 'with one bound he was free'.

On this morning I retraced my steps to the village of Brae, then turned left onto the minor road that led up the edge of Sullom Voe towards the little car ferry to Yell. There was a stiff northerly breeze in my face and it was cold. There was no traffic in either direction and as the oil terminal came into distant view it was all rather depressing. I cycled past the end of the runway serving the terminal, and, near knots of airport buildings, I could see a line of big yellow Chinook helicopters waiting to take off. I could even see the passengers, all wearing orange life jackets, looking out of the windows. As I was wearing a bright yellow Berghaus jacket and was the only moving object in a barren landscape, I felt self-conscious. The big whirling choppers lumbered into the sky and headed off towards the North Sea rigs. I could visualise myself getting smaller and smaller and wondered if the oil workers were thinking, 'Where's that stupid bugger down there think he's going?'

At the side of the road, a big plaque announces a few basic statistics about the oil industry, all pretty forgettable unless you are interested, except for one. I was informed that the oil stored in each one of the giant cylindrical containers would be used up in Britain in a single day. The trouble was, I didn't know whether to marvel at how much or how little this was.

By now I was riding with gritted teeth. It all seemed to be imperceptibly uphill and the headwind was sapping both strength and willpower. I prayed for the sight of the car ferry and at last freewheeled down a graceful bend into Tofts Voe just as a little toy-town ferry hove into sight. I found a tiny cabin for passengers that kept me out of the wind blowing down Yell Sound.

Twenty minutes later the ferry docked at Bigga, a tiny collection of houses and a general store where I could buy a can of Lucozade and something to eat. I was learning quickly that you need a high fluid intake and that if you don't eat and drink you can experience a huge energy drop very quickly, much more quickly, I thought, than on mountain walks.

I decided to ride up the west side of Yell. On the map the road seemed straighter and maybe it would be more sheltered than the eastern route, which took in something called the Hill of Reafirth, which didn't sound much fun. But neither, I soon found, was the western route, though the endless views across Yell Sound were spectacular. There was a really long hill on the road as well and, after riding a brand new bike for only three days, all the cables were stretching. Consequently, the gears kept slipping, particularly in the lowest ratios, and I was reduced to evil temper as the chain hopped about of its own accord whenever I applied pressure. Climbing up one bend I was reduced to apoplectic fury as it happened again. 'Oh, for fu–!' I was cut off in mid-sentence by a sign which actually said 'Mid Yell', and I burst out laughing. Is there a figure of speech, I wondered, to cope with this phenomenon? Roadside tautology perhaps, or maybe locative onomatopaeia?

More practically, the sign did indicate the proximity of civilisation of some description and I suddenly had another minor brainwave. If I could find a bed and breakfast here, I could; a) have a bath or shower, which I needed; b) get a night's sleep in a proper bed; and c) (the cunning bit) leave everything here and ride up to Muckle Flugga unladen and back again the same day, which would easily solve the problems of getting back to Lerwick.

Mid Yell was a tiny collection of windswept houses with distant views of the islands of Hascosay and Fetlar. Closer at hand I was delighted to see that the view included a general store, and what looked suspiciously like a pub, or its nearest Scottish equivalent, a bar. The man in the store directed me to a house about fifty yards away which did bed and breakfast. Within minutes I had met Peter and Catherine Gibb. Catherine showed me a room with a splendid double bed and a bathroom with an equally splendid bath. Even better was the news that Peter was the owner of the bar, which was also a restaurant. What's more, Catherine asked if there was any washing I needed doing. Sometimes happiness can be found in very simple things.

Later, washed, shaved and wearing clean underwear, I strolled down to the bar where Peter made me an impressive plate of fish and chips followed, I regret to say, by a magnificent chocolate fudge cake. Burping contentedly after a couple of pints, I dragged myself back to my room and within seconds, dropped into a dreamless sleep. I woke five minutes later – except that it wasn't. It was next morning and I'd just learned the first cruel fact of B&B'ing on a cycling tour, which is that you are paying good money for oblivion. I felt cheated and mildly annoyed. I'd just slept my money away!

Breakfast was wonderful. Two giant duck eggs, each containing enough cholesterol to block the arteries of an elephant, with as much toast and coffee as I could manage (quite a lot actually). Catherine was the head teacher of a tiny school on Unst and soon left to drive up to the ferry that took her to work each day. I followed at a more leisurely pace, riding again into a brisk head-wind past long freshly dug peat cuttings. The peat itself was stacked in slabs to dry before being used as fuel. The peat bore an uncanny resemblance to the chocolate fudge cake of the night before, which made me feel just a tad nauseous on top of my excessive breakfast.

The crossing to Unst takes only about ten minutes. Then it was head down for Herma Ness and Muckle Flugga. A few patches of watery sunlight lit up the windswept moorland. Though Unst was visually much the same as Yell and the mainland, it did feel as though I was cycling off the edge of the world, especially as I passed a small brewery set on its own called the Valhalla. Beyond this was an unprepossessing row of houses called Baltasound, and it was here that I chalked up my first hundred miles before cycling the last few miles to the road end.

My map marked a coastal path round the edge of Herma Ness but it was obvious that a bigger and better path went over the top of the hill. It seemed a bit odd to be walking and my legs felt remarkably weak. It was only about two miles to the top of the hill, which could easily have been anywhere in the Pennines, had it not been for the mass of wheeling gulls and the odd skua eyeing me balefully. As the latter were not yet guarding their eggs they made no move to attack me. On Hoy and St Kilda I had grown wary of these powerful, aggressive birds that come at you out of the sun. I had learned to carry an umbrella or long stick to ward them off, but here it was unnecessary.

As I walked over the flat top of the hill, which by now I couldn't help thinking of as 'Herman Hess', I at last saw the reef of rocks on which the Muckle Flugga Lighthouse is built. I walked down until I could see clear water between the shore and the rocks. Time for a photo, I thought, and took a self-portrait on my little automatic Canon Sureshot. Muckle Flugga was one of the many Stevenson family lighthouses illuminating the wilder Scottish extremities and built at great hazard 150 years ago. This one was superintended by Robert Louis's uncle David who advised Trinity House against building on the most northerly point of the British Isles but was overruled because the Admiralty needed a light to guide naval convoys to the Crimea. The stone of the rock itself fractured too easily to be used in the construction so it is one of the few lighthouses made of brick. Beyond the lighthouse the next point of any note would be the North Pole. I had completed my first real objective but my journey was only just starting. At the top of the hill I realised that the north wind had dropped. Looking homewards, I could see sunlight reflecting off dozens of little lochs and the first gentle breath of wind blew in my face – from the south.

4

Serenaded by a Snipe

By the time I had cycled back to the Yell ferry, it was late in the afternoon. Catherine Gibb, on her way home from school, pulled up in her little car beside me. 'Sorry I can't give you a lift, but I'll make sure the hot water's on for a bath.' When the ferry docked on the other side she drove off, leaving me with only a sore bum and a headwind to accompany me the remaining few miles. As I freewheeled down the last long hill before the turn-off to Mid Yell, I allowed myself the first real feeling of satisfaction. Maybe this whole daft idea would actually come to fruition – eventually.

After a repeat performance of the previous night (including the pudding) I awoke in a very good mood, made better by another huge overload of cholesterol and a prowl round Peter's Aladdin's Cave of a garage. Several nuts and bolts from the panniers and mudguards had either fallen off or shaken loose. These I replaced or tightened and I also managed to adjust the tension on the gears, though it still wasn't perfect.

The weather on the other hand was; far better than the previous days, with strong sunlight and only a few puffy clouds blowing, needless to say, from the south. I left Catherine and Peter reluctantly, with many thanks for their generous hospitality, and promptly took the wrong turning out of Mid Yell. I had intended to go back along the east side of the island and thought that the turn-off was a couple of miles down the road. When I realised it was actually just outside the house I'd left, I couldn't face going back, so I retraced my earlier route to the ferry at Bigga, this time

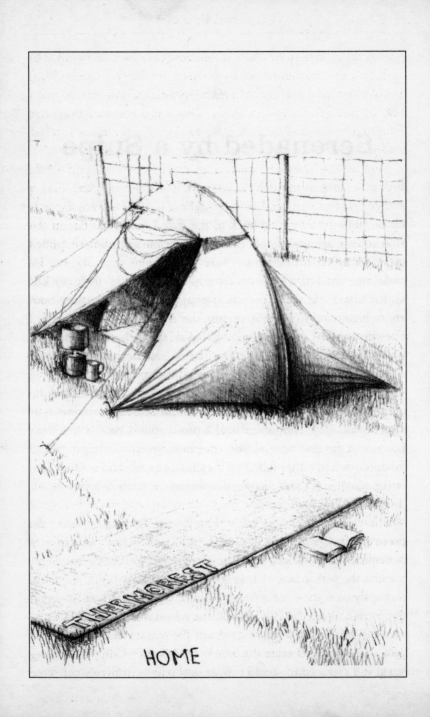

HOME

getting quite stupendous panoramic views across Yell Sound. The vast sky and turquoise ocean seemed to pulsate like a Mark Rothko painting and the Mainland (Shetland that is) was just a blur of pale green between them. This was the sort of thing that I had come for and I revelled in the joy of movement through sunlight and colour.

Back on the Mainland (and going the right way) I found for the first time, and to my delight, that I could lapse into the kind of trance I had experienced so often on long walks. I am not trying to claim anything even vaguely mystical, but I found quite regularly that from mid- to late afternoon I went into a mildly euphoric state, in which time distance and effort seemed to slip by unnoticed, even when it rained. I could somehow drift away into whatever reverie took my fancy, or become absorbed in the ever-changing views. Cycling, I decided, is the ideal means of transport through the British Isles. Walking would be too slow and laborious and driving far too quick. In the 1970s 1 had driven overland to India and found most of it interminably boring, even though we did the journey in less than two weeks. Occasionally we had passed a long-distance cyclist doggedly pedalling through the deserts of Iran and Afghanistan. The sight always filled me with horror. More recently the wonderfully eccentric Swedish climber, Goran Kropp, had cycled from his home to Kathmandu and walked from there, carrying all his kit, to solo Everest with no support at all. Then (and here's the bit that really impressed me) he cycled all the way back to Sweden. By his standards my ride was trivial to the point of non-existence and I found it almost impossible to conceive of the amount of willpower and self-discipline necessary for him to carry it out.

Back in the present I suddenly found myself cycling into Voe, at the junction with the road branching off to Mavis Grind, where I started looking for a place to camp. For some reason I got quite picky and rejected several possible sites before I slipped down a steep side road and found a tiny quarry with a flat, if rather stony floor. A Shetland farmer of advanced years, on whose land it was, stopped in a clapped-out Land Rover. I assumed it was to tell me to find somewhere else. Instead it was to suggest I pitched my tent in a nearby field. It would be more comfortable but didn't have such a lovely view across to Olna Firth. I explained I was quite happy to camp in the quarry and we had a long, if one-sided conversation on the subject of global warming, about which he seemed extremely concerned. The trouble was I couldn't decide whether he thought it existed or whether he believed it was all a media conspiracy. Just as I was convinced he was a fully signed-up member of Friends of the Earth, he would pour scorn on the gullibility of people who believed everything they read in the papers. Within minutes, though, he would ask me searching questions about rainfall levels in Derbyshire and how strange and worrying the weather patterns had been over the last five years. In the end I didn't know what either of us thought.

After my evening meal (chicken curry à la Curran) I sat alternately looking at the evening light and reading my latest book. I had finished *Memoirs of a Geisha* that my daughter Becky had given and with which, to my surprise, I had become completely captivated. Now I was reading Nicholas Shakespeare's excellent biography of the eccentric travel writer and novelist, Bruce Chatwin. I had read just about everything Chatwin had written in his short life and found him fascinating, compelling and also mildly irritating. I was intrigued to read that Chatwin left many of the people he visited furious both with his sweeping assertions and sometimes cruel dismissals after accepting their hospitality. He never spent very long in any one place and often tried to bend his observations to fit his anthropological theories – in particular the concept of man as being basically nomadic; it was an attractive theory for an inherent wastrel like me but I wasn't convinced. I was amused that Chatwin deluded himself that he travelled light, carrying only an ancient hand-stitched leather rucksack, an item of baggage that seemed to have great symbolic significance for him. In fact he invariably travelled with huge amounts of excess baggage as well, and I couldn't resist a smirk as I thought of the times I had arrived at Heathrow to see Chris Bonington unloading a Volvo Estate and watched awe-struck as a pile of rucksacks, kitbags, cameras, satellite phones and computers mounted. Invariably, all this would have occurred just after a press conference in which Chris had extolled the virtues of lightweight Alpine-style expeditions!

I dropped off to sleep that night, pleased that all I had to do the next day was pedal gently back to Lerwick. There was no hurry and the ferry to Stromness didn't leave until midday the day after. I could even have a lie in, though of course this rarely works when you are camping, particularly when it's fine and the sun hits the tent at some unearthly hour. I was awake soon after seven and too hot shortly after that, even though it was still quite chilly outside. At least I was getting some semblance of order in packing up, not that it mattered much in good weather but it would in driving rain, which would arrive any day now, I thought.

Of course on the ride back I did not find my repair outfit at the spot where I had adjusted the gears on the way out, but I did hit over 40 miles an hour as I freewheeled down the long hill into Lerwick. This frightened me considerably and I never dared go as fast again. On the way into town I stopped at a garage that hired bikes and found on the first floor a comprehensive bike shop with spares of every kind. I replaced the tool kit, for half the cost of the lost one. I was also directed to one of the few designated campsites in the Shetlands.

This was in the grounds of a leisure centre on the outskirts of Lerwick and, like many of the campsites I was to visit in the coming weeks, was primarily organised for caravans. The leisure centre itself was complete with swimming pool, gymnasiums, saunas, cafeteria, drink machines, and all the various trappings designed to offset any good from the exercise you've just taken.

I had to answer some bewildering questions and then leave a

huge lavatory deposit. I will rephrase that. I had to pay five pounds (refundable) for a key to the gentlemen's toilet. My designated site was just outside it and was big enough for a circus tent. I felt stupid pitching my tiny one-man shelter, particularly as I was the only occupant of the entire site which was surrounded by roads and tall sodium lights. I felt that my last night in the Shetlands lacked romance. For the first time since leaving Sheffield I locked my bike to a drainpipe on the aforementioned toilet block. I was very tempted to push off into Lerwick and find a decent meal somewhere, but knew that tomorrow I'd be on the ferry and then in Stromness, which would involve at least two bought meals. So I resisted temptation and made a rather messy spag bog while I lost myself in the life of Bruce Chatwin, who would not have been seen dead in a leisure centre campsite, even as the sole occupant.

With the combination of nearby streetlights and the fact that it didn't stay dark for long, I didn't sleep well and kept waking to a peculiar noise like a wound-up elastic band unwinding. The noise was repeated all around me at infrequent intervals. I was intrigued and kept looking out of the tent into the murky pre-dawn light. The noise persisted and I couldn't see what was causing it. At last I could just make out a bird zigzagging around the campsite but couldn't work out how it was making the noise. A couple of weeks later I was talking to an ornithologist outside the Dundonnell Hotel, who told me it was a snipe. Apparently it makes the noise by vibrating its tail feathers during display-flight. I couldn't help wondering why it was doing this in the middle of the night when any element of display would be absent without X-ray vision. It was certainly noisy enough but I was apparently its only audience.

In the morning I reclaimed my deposit and mooched around Lerwick until it was time for the ferry. As I wheeled my bike into the bowels of the ship I was joined by a couple of cyclists. They were just about the first I had met and I greeted them with some trepidation. I could guess what was coming. They were English but living on Shetland and off for a week's cycling holiday. The woman had previously done John O'Groats to Land's End in some ludicrously fast time – a week, I seem to remember – and she was very, very into bikes. Sure enough, within minutes I was fending off quick-fire questions about why I had chosen various bits and pieces of bike technology. My feeble defence that I hadn't chosen them at all, was met with incomprehension.

I started to feel the same sense of inferiority as I do in TV companies and climbing shops, and reverted to the same tactics I use in them, which is to start bullshitting about something else. Here, it was quite simple and the 'I'm not really a cyclist – I climb and make TV documentaries' gambit was played until the bike inquisition ceased. I made a mental note that next time I was questioned about digital TV camcorders to deflect the conversation into gear ratios and saddle soreness.

Sometimes I wonder how long I'll get away with my technical deficiencies and can imagine a nightmare scenario being quizzed in court by a computer expert, a still photographer, a climbing gear manufacturer and a small child who can programme a video recorder. 'M'lud, the accused has spent thirty-five years of his life living a lie. The only thing he seems to know anything about at all is the out-of-date technology of building balsa wood model aircraft circa 1954–57. And even that only applies to gliders and rubber-band-powered biplanes'. Apart from that, the cycling couple were nice enough, but I didn't fancy six hours of evasive manoeuvring and so I spent most of the voyage down to Stromness hiding behind Bruce Chatwin.

The ferry slid into Stromness as dusk fell. The *St Ola*, the car ferry to the Scottish mainland, was still occupying the ferry berth, so in a maritime version of stacking we were taken down the coast for a spin around the towering cliffs of St John's Head and the Old Man of Hoy, both lit a lurid orange in the evening sky. Here I am again, I thought, realising that this would be my fourth visit to this famous landmark. I also remembered that I had two reasons for being here, one of which I wasn't looking forward to.

As the ferry berthed the light was fading and so was my resolve to camp. It was a cold evening and the campsite, which the ferry passed on its way to dock, was predictably deserted. So I settled for another B&B, persuading myself that this would be the last for some time. When I had found one and got all my gear off the bike, it was too late for the decent meal I had been promising myself and I settled for a ghastly fish supper. I ate it on the pavement outside the chip shop in the congenial company of a couple of severely inebriated Orcadians and a gaggle of teenagers engaged in the time-honoured courtship ritual of throwing chips at each other. As they appeared to have been fried in black axle grease (the chips, not the teenagers), it seemed as good a use for them as any. Time for bed, I thought.

5

Back to Hoy

The little motor boat ferrying foot passengers and one cyclist chugged across the blue waters of Hoy Sound, skirting the island of Graemsay into Burra Sound. I was talking to three young American students spending a year at St Andrew's University. They were visiting Hoy for the day and I told them about the old scuttled wreck in Burra Sound which had been a famous landmark as you approached Hoy. But, to my slight embarrassment, there was no sign of it and I found out later that it had finally broken up in the previous winter's gales. As we drew into the jetty in the Bay of Creekland, it was a glorious spring day with a bank of mist fast lifting over St John's Head.

My plans for the next couple of days depended on whom I would find at the farmhouse above Rackwick Bay run by Jack and Dorothy Rendall. For many years they had provided unstinting hospitality for visiting climbers taking on the spectacular challenge of one of Britain's most photographed and televised sea stacks, the Old Man of Hoy. I had first stayed there in 1994 to film Mike Banks who, at the age of seventy-two, climbed the Old Man for charity. Before that I had camped near an old bothy when I had climbed it myself with Paul Nunn and Phil Kershaw in 1983. Then in 1997 I had returned for a much more ambitious project. But now, as I cycled up the little road between the two biggest hills on Hoy, Ward Hill and the Knap of Trowieglen, I was delighted just to be back again. The last of the mist dispersed and in brilliant sunshine I freewheeled gently down the road as the lovely

RACKWICK BAY

vista of Rackwick Bay framed by red sandstone cliffs hove into
sight. As I pedalled up the last steep rise to the farm and youth
hostel the tall rangy figure of Jack Rendall appeared. He looked
surprised to see me again, this time on a bike and on my own, and
I asked him if there was any sign of Mike Banks.

'He left not half an hour ago.' My heart sank a bit at the news.
'But you should catch him at the Old Man.'

'Oh, great – when did he arrive?'

'Only last night.'

Even better. I had known for some time that Mike, now seventy-
seven, was returning yet again to climb the Old Man for charity
and to ensure that his 'oldest man on the Old Man' title remained
intact. I always enjoyed the company of Mike and his wife Pat and
knew if I timed it right their presence would lighten a sad task.

I was here primarily because a great friend and mentor, Chris
Lister, had died in 1999. He and I had worked together for over
twenty years on various film projects, including the first
Himalayan venture on the Trango Tower in 1976, the Kongur
expedition in 1981 with Chris Bonington and, most memorably,
the harrowing K2 film made after the disastrous events of 1986.
For all the film proposals the TV companies took up, there were
many more that never got off the ground. I had been to see him
one day in 1995 to discuss my latest crop of ideas, none of which
had impressed him overmuch.

'The trouble is you believe in them and I quite like them but
how are we going to sell them to a cynical commissioning editor?
Why can't you think of a nice simple idea that everyone can grasp
instantly?' Irritated, because I knew Chris was right, I bridled. 'I
suppose you mean something like Catherine Destivelle soloing the
Old Man of Hoy.'

We looked at each other, then both burst out laughing. Bingo.

Over the last ten years I had met perhaps the world's best known
female climber, Catherine Destivelle, on three or four occasions,

but it was at the 1994 Dundee Mountain Film Festival that we first
got to talk about working together. Catherine had just returned
from Kathmandu and had flown to Paris, then Edinburgh. She was
overtired and jet-lagged, but she topped the bill at Dundee and
gave a stunning film and slide show that entranced the capacity
audience. Afterwards, over a drink, I probably put my foot in it by
saying that I thought it was time she made a film that did more than
just show her as a sexy rock athlete soloing well-rehearsed climbs.
Stupidly, I told her I was fed up with the endless French soft porn
videos, where bronzed gods or goddesses posed half-naked on the
vertical limestone of the Verdon Gorge. This went down like a lead
balloon, as I remembered, too late, that Catherine's first film was
just such a work. Nevertheless I ploughed on and told her that one
day we'd make a film we would both be proud of. Catherine, always
polite and charming, giggled, 'We'll see.'

Once Chris Lister and I had hatched our little film project, we
swung into action to make it happen – a lot easier said than done.
I rang Catherine in France to ask if she would be interested ('Why
not?') and sent her a few photos, articles and guidebook descrip-
tions while Chris played the gigantic Rubik's Cube of fitting deals
together to make it happen. It took until 1997 for everything to
slot into place and then it developed the momentum of a rocket.
I was only just back from Tibet when a phone call from Chris
Lister told me that a) the film was on; b) it was to be shot in about
ten days' time; and c) I would be picking up Catherine and her
husband Erik Decamp at Glasgow airport and driving them up to
the ferry at Thurso. Bloody hell. Chris had actually pulled it off.

Which was all very well, except that I hadn't even unpacked my
gear from Tibet, some of which was still in transit and, more to
the point, I hadn't done any rock-climbing at all that year. Not
that I would be expected to perform at a high level, or even a low
one, but there is no doubt that even jumaring into camera position
on a rock-climbing film is sometimes quite daunting, and I was
under no illusions that to shoot an hour documentary about

Catherine soloing on the Old Man of Hoy in just one week would be quite a challenge.

As Chris rang off he added one more thing. 'Oh, by the way, the reason we've got to get this done quickly is because she's pregnant.'

By the time I pulled into the rainswept car park at Glasgow airport I was a bag of nerves. What would happen if we didn't get on? Supposing Catherine and Erik hated the whole concept? Supposing – God, I could hardly bear to think of it, but Geoff Birtles had spelled it out before I left Sheffield: 'Just remember if anything happens to Catherine, the climbing world will never forgive you.' He was joking, sort of.

I was half an hour early. Scanning the arrivals board, I realised I had reverted to the very small child I remembered standing outside a house where I had been invited for a children's party. My mother had pushed me inside and left me on the verge of tears of embarrassment and shyness. Now look here, Curran, this is quite absurd – you've just been to Tibet with Sir Christian Bonington, no less. You've made God knows how many films. You know you'll get on fine with Catherine and Erik – why on earth are you thinking like this?

Suddenly the tall blond figure of Erik appeared pushing a trolley overloaded with holdall and rucksacks. Behind him strolled a small figure in faded jeans, trainers and a stylish black down jacket, a shock of dark wavy hair and the famous flashing toothy smile. I noticed she was limping slightly.

'How's the leg?'' I knew she had broken it the year before in Antarctica.

'Not so bad, but I 'ave a problem with inflammation on my hip – okay for climbing though.' And another big grin. I relaxed a bit.

During the rest of the drive up to Thurso Catherine rather casually broke the news to me that this would be the first film she had ever been involved with that wasn't her own idea. Great news, I thought gloomily – now it's all my fault if things don't work out.

Why didn't I think wow, what blind faith she must have in my incredible imagination and judgement? Do I need to ask?

The first view of the Old Man from the ferry was unpromising: it disappeared into low cloud and was only just visible in driving rain and mist. Catherine and Erik came on deck and dutifully commented to the camera while I couldn't help wondering, if the weather stayed as foul as this, whether there would be any film at all. Meanwhile I felt seasick and prayed for land.

Early next morning we started carrying monster loads from the youth hostel at Rackwick Bay to the cliff-top overlooking the stack. Reasonably fit from Tibet, I carried a gigantic sack that threatened to make my kneecaps explode. But it was only about forty-five minutes' walk and most of it flat. Cubby Cuthbertson and John Whittle, our safety team, had decided, quite rightly, that the precarious descent down the muddy path that weaves its way to the foot of the Old Man was potentially dangerous for non-climbers and put in a line of fixed rope all the way down. I was instantly impressed, for many experienced climbers find it hard to imagine that easy ground like this could be a death trap for the tired inexperienced film crew who were always carrying awkward loads up and down.

Catherine and Erik meanwhile had decided that they would climb the normal route together, just to see what it was like. Catherine was slightly concerned: 'I do not know this climb – I don't know the rock and I don't know how I will like it.' Sitting at the bottom in driving wind and spitting rain, I couldn't imagine that she would be terribly enamoured of the tottering pile of lichenous sandstone that towered over her.

I had my own little Sony digital video camera with me which I intended to use on the climb. Given the vagaries of the weather we felt that we should film everything as it happened. Discovery Channel was going to use the film in their series called *The Professionals* and part of our brief was to show how climbing films are made (or possibly not made, I thought). Hardly had I got the camera ready when Catherine shot up the first easy pitch, not bothering to put any runners in. She climbed so fast it was actually quite hard to film her. I was impressed.

The Old Man of Hoy now has something like nine routes up its four faces and arêtes. The original route, first climbed by Tom Patey, Rusty Baillie and Chris Bonington in 1966, is the easiest, but still has tremendous character. First a rather loose set of broken walls leads to a big ledge from which you get a good view of the first part of the second pitch. This provides the crux and consists of a wide crack, at one point almost a chimney that cuts through two overhangs. It is hard to grade the pitch and even harder to climb it elegantly. Above this the climbing is much easier for about 200 feet to the foot of a final corner crack. Here the rock is sound and the climbing straightforward. It is probably the most enjoyable pitch on the Old Man.

Catherine meanwhile had made light work of the second pitch and soon both she and Erik disappeared from view. I knew our other cameraman, Gavin Crowther, would be getting long shots from the cliff top, so there wasn't a great deal of point in my sitting around at the bottom but I felt it would be rather rude to desert my post on the first day, and settled down to wait for their return. This happened surprisingly quickly. First Catherine abseiled down the second pitch and half climbed, half swung on the rope back to the big ledge. The wind had increased and through the camera lens the ropes blew wildly. Then Erik followed. Halfway down he unclipped the abseil ropes from the back of the corner and to my amazement and delight made an enormous (if unintentional) swing almost out of the camera frame. He came swooping back and then swung out again. It was a completely unexpected shot but it was exactly what was needed to give the first brief sequence a bit of drama. Then Catherine descended the first pitch with the ropes streaming out near horizontally behind her. She arrived almost at my feet.

'Did you get to the top?'

'Yes – of course – not too difficult, but the second pitch is too dangerous, too much, how do you say, sandy? – a bit shitty. The rest I can do easily, but the second pitch – no, too dangerous.'

This news was not unexpected. Indeed I was surprised that in the conditions she was prepared to solo any of the Old Man at all, but I had always thought that the second pitch would be a problem. Catherine, of course, could and had soloed far harder things than this but there was a world of difference between hot, dry continental rock-climbs and being faced with the bleak, damp, birdshit-spattered sandstone of Hoy. Now, she explained, she would use a back-rope and self-belay up the pitch. In many ways this was a bonus. I certainly felt happier about us filming her on the pitch and it meant that, as she belayed, we could do lots of big close-up sequences in relative safety. Even a scene explaining her self-belaying system would add interest and a bit of tension to the film.

In the evening gloom we strolled back to the hostel. Now we had a day's filming under our belts, I felt emotionally committed and fully charged. All my earlier doubts had evaporated and I sensed that everyone was beginning to think that we might be on a winner.

That evening, Catherine, who had been interviewed at length earlier in the day, was in expansive mood and told us quite unself-consciously what it was like to be famous. Most British climbers cannot conceive of the publicity Catherine gets in France, where she has the same sort of public profile as a pop star, fashion model or tennis player. Some of the fame she obviously enjoyed, but the downside, being mobbed in the street and above all, being touched by strangers, she loathed. Occasionally she had suffered verbal abuse by people who felt they knew her and she hadn't responded in the way they'd imagined she should. I sensed she really enjoyed getting away from it all to the British climbing scene which is less prone to adulation. I remembered her the previous year in a Sheffield pub, a pint in one hand and a guilty cigarette in the other, chatting away next to a group of climbers who almost pointedly ignored her.

The next four days were long and the weather was marginal at best, but Catherine was superb. She was professional, calm, confident, co-operative, and fun to work with. Before she started the crucial second pitch Catherine explained to me her system of self-belaying as I filmed her. She tied one end of the rope to the many in-place pitons on the stance at the top of the first pitch. This then ran through a gri-gri, a sophisticated version of the jumar clamp that was attached to her harness, and would lock the rope if she fell. The rest of the rope ran in a long loop below her with the other end also attached to her in case her system failed. Every time she moved up she would have to pull enough slack through the gri-gri to complete the next few moves. She would protect the pitch in the normal way, though she actually used very few runners. She was the first to admit it was not a system she would recommend to anyone else and, to my amazement, when demonstrating the gri-gri, she couldn't remember how to thread the rope through. Through giggles she got it right and then, with a big grin to the camera, said, 'I do not want to die.' When she had climbed the pitch she would unrope leaving everything in place until she returned. She carried a spare rope for abseiling in a small daysack. Gavin Crowther, to my secret delight, had boundless enthusiasm for jumaring, having done a lot of work in caves, filming with Sid Perou. So on the frightening second pitch he would hang high in the groove filming down, while I leant out at the bottom and filmed Catherine as she climbed across the first traverse and up the initial overhang. My perch was perfect, as I could actually stand on a tiny ledge right on the edge of the buttress and shoot down and across.

I shared the stance for much of the day, first with safety man John Whittle, then with Erik, who as a Chamonix guide by profession, observed all these goings on with sympathy, tact and good advice. He had a supply of dry one-liners, and was great company, not just for Catherine but all of us. I could see that he was the perfect guide: encouraging, safety-conscious, and always willing to lend a hand in mundane chores.

On the third day the weather was so awful that it was decided to do an extended interview with Catherine and Erik inside the crofter's cottage which served as a tiny museum at Rackwick Bay. Gavin would film this while I forced myself to walk along the coastal path and up to St John's Head, where I knew from my last trip with Mike Banks that there was an unusual view along the cliffs looking down on the Old Man. Then I had taken a series of slides that had a strange, rather Japanese feel to them, in the simple juxtaposition of cliff, stack, sun and sea. Today the weather was dreadful, with high winds and violent squalls, and where I had stood before the path had disappeared, leaving an ugly scar of fresh earth and boulders sliding into a huge abyss. Had my first visit contributed to its losing battle with gravity? Dubiously, I unpacked camera and tripod and framed the Old Man in the same way as I had done with the stills camera. But today there was no sunlight glinting through the heat haze, just a blurred set of grey forms against a lowering sky. I hung around for over an hour, shooting whenever I felt the light improved a bit. But I was not impressed. Damp, disappointed and tired, I plodded back to the hostel. Later, I was surprised and delighted to find our editor, Barry Reynolds, using the shots several times as cutaways. They actually looked much better than I had thought and I realised that I had been making comparisons with the memories of the still shots, which was quite pointless. In any case, the subdued colours worked perfectly with the rest of the film.

An increasing worry throughout the week was getting helicopter shots. Our budget only ran to a couple of hours' use, though we had some flexibility as to when to use them. It was vital to get shots of Catherine on top and comprehensive coverage of angles up, down and around the stack. But the wind and poor visibility foiled us until Thursday, when we had to order the thing, come what may.

On that day, Catherine, who had already soloed the route several times, was to climb it entirely on her own without camera and safety crews getting in the way of long shots from the helicopter. The weather was still miserable but the wind had dropped a bit. A photographer from *Paris Match* had turned up to cover the climb for his magazine. He was charming, urbane, spoke excellent English and understood that our film had priority. Nevertheless, his presence was just one more complication. By mid-afternoon the weather brightened up and Catherine set off on her own. On the second pitch she seemed to be struggling a bit, then announced through her radio mike, 'It is wet, very wet. I dunno why.' This was strange because it hadn't actually rained at all that day. We could only suppose that the downpours of the previous days had drained from the upper section of the Old Man and funnelled into the back of the crack. I couldn't help feeling a bit of a thrill though, as I filmed her cursing in French and repeating, '*Merde*. It's very dangerous.' Just what we wanted.

To my delight, as Catherine set off on the easier middle pitches, I heard the first faint smacking of rotor blades which soon grew to a crescendo as the chopper suddenly appeared over the headland and, after a quick circuit around the top of the Old Man it landed next to the film crew on the cliff top. Quite soon it appeared again and started several slow manoeuvres, with Gavin filming from the space where the passenger door would have been, if it hadn't just been removed. Gavin had done a lot of filming from helicopters and knew exactly what to do, which basically is to keep the camera still and make the pilot do the work.

By now Catherine was out of my sight high on the Old Man, so I packed up my gear and climbed back up the path to the point where Nick Lyons was patiently and unobtrusively doing his soundman's job, as he had done all week. Festooned with cables, booms, mikes and headphones, Nick epitomised the soundrecordist – mildly eccentric, forever tinkering with gadgets. I can never decide whether they have a natural ability to improvise or whether they are prone to breaking things in the first place. Nick was also a professional Yorkshireman; by which I mean he was in the honourable line of mildly batty figures like cricket umpire Dickie Bird, Geoff Boycott, Michael Parkinson and Fred Truman, all of whom hail from Barnsley or very near to it, and all manage to bring any subject back to their beloved county within minutes of any topic of conversation being introduced.

Earlier in the week Nick, who insisted on wearing an ex-British-Rail orange nylon cagoule and overtrousers and steel-capped boots, was standing, shaking with cold, at the foot of the Old Man, pointing his boom mike skywards for hours on end. Our director became concerned.

'Nick – get out of the wind before you become an exposure case.'

Nick turned to me: 'Nearest place out of t'wind from here is Pontefract.'

One evening we saw him in earnest conversation with Catherine who, being pregnant, had acquired some curious eating habits. After a long conversation with Nick, she asked me, ''Oo is this 'Arry Ramsden?' To be fair to Nick, she did have quite a thing about fish and chips.

By the time I arrived at Nick's grassy eyrie, Catherine was waiting on the last stance for the go ahead to climb the final corner. I have to admit that, even having climbed the pitch before and knowing that it isn't difficult, I still hated seeing Catherine on her own on the Old Man. She was trying to keep warm on the ledge and at one point did some bouldering moves on the wall behind her. Ridiculously, I could hardly bear to watch, and Geoff Birtles's words of warning came back to me. At last we got the green light. The helicopter hovered, plunged and zoomed round her and every camera rolled.

As Catherine climbed the last moves I'm afraid a lump came to my throat. The tiny figure topped out and then stood waving to the helicopter and the cliff-top crew. Behind her a ray of watery sunshine lit up the sea. It was the first sunshine we'd seen all week. I rushed up to the top of the approach path and ran round to the headland directly opposite the top of the Old Man. I had all the video footage I wanted but I did want a nice still of Catherine on top. I was lucky; I got Catherine with helicopter, Catherine without, Catherine with sun and Catherine in silhouette. Great. Just then the chopper came back and landed. I wondered if he'd pick Catherine up from the top but she was adamant she would abseil down and remove her gear from the second pitch herself. I suspected there was a reason for this. When she had made her new route on the West Face of the Dru in 1991 she had allowed herself the luxury of a flight down from the summit and had been heavily criticised by the French media who felt that she hadn't made a complete ascent. Despite having climbed – and descended – the route several times, I suspected that she felt a ride in the helicopter could be misreported.

The pilot chatted for a few minutes as he replaced the door. 'I can take one of you back to Rackwick. Anyone want a lift?'

John Whittle and Erik were standing nearby and both really deserved it, but Erik kindly insisted I should get the ride. I remember as a small boy being allowed to go on the footplate of a steam train. I felt much the same as the pilot did the equivalent of a handbrake turn round the Old Man. I had reeling images of cliffs, sea and sky, with a fleeting glimpse of Catherine in mid-abseil. Then he gunned it, seemingly straight at the cliff, climbing steeply. We shot over the top to see Erik, John and the others waving, before skimming low over the path back to Rackwick. Five minutes later I stood in the field behind the hostel listening to the faint clatter of the helicopter as it sped off towards the mainland. Suddenly it was very quiet. What a curious end to the day. I went into the silent hostel and put the kettle on.

Friday was the last day of shooting and in addition to getting a

comprehensive set of close-ups of hands and feet and cutaways of
cormorants, seals, puffins etc., we had to lug every bit of gear back
to the hostel. Unwilling to do the trip more than once, we all
carried gigantic loads. Halfway we had one last scene to film. One
of the more alarming facts of life on Orkney is running the
gauntlet of the arctic skua, who, when defending its nest, is a
highly aggressive bird. Naturally when we wanted to film an
attack it didn't happen and Catherine and Erik had to wander off
the path looking for trouble. They didn't have to walk far and the
big brown bird came swooping out of the sky, skimming just over
their heads, or in a frontal attack, flying low towards them and
only pulling up at the very last second to whistle past with a
warning shriek. I remembered being attacked the first time I had
come here and thought Catherine and Erik were being extraordinarily conscientious to do this for the camera, particularly as
Catherine hated sea birds.

With this scene in the can we had actually finished shooting. To
celebrate, the sun came out properly, and Cubby took a super
picture of a smiling Catherine and Erik, lit by the evening light
with the cliffs of Rackwick in the background. It was the only
photo on the whole trip taken in full sunlight.

Chris Lister was determined that we celebrate in style on the
last evening and had booked a table for eleven at the only restaurant on Hoy. It turned out to be a huge room, entirely empty
except for our table. It reminded me of a school canteen. The
waitress stood by shyly, a bit forlorn.

'Um, can we see the wine list?'

She looked stricken: 'We have only ten bottles in at the
moment.'

'Oh well, better bring 'em all out.'

Amidst the Liebfraumilch and Valpolicella were a couple
of bottles that at least claimed to have some kind of French
origin and we pushed them down to Catherine and Erik and the
ever-suave *Paris Match* man; God knows what he was thinking.

The meal was okay in a basic Scottish kind of way and we were determined to relax and enjoy it. Suddenly, to my horror, Chris called for silence and announced that, as the whole exercise was my fault and I was used to after-dinner speaking, I'd better stand up and say a few words. I was nonplussed. I couldn't think of anything to say at all. Then, from the furthest recesses of my mind came a story I had once read of a banquet given in, I think, the Lycée Palace by General de Gaulle for Harold Macmillan, presumably after some grim diplomatic negotiations over the Common Market had gone wrong. Apparently, after one particularly chilly silence Dorothy Macmillan had leant across to Madame de Gaulle and asked her what she thought what was the most important thing in life? 'A penis,' Madame replied with conviction. There was a thunderstruck silence. Then General de Gaulle came to the rescue. 'She means 'appiness.' I recounted this and proposed a toast: 'To 'appiness' and sat down quickly. Erik told me that his only regret was that the story wouldn't translate into French. Catherine, when she occasionally rings up from France still giggles and wishes me it.

The finished film was a great success and is still frequently shown on the Discovery Channel. It led directly to a much longer commission to film the second Sepu Kangri expedition in 1998. Throughout its post-production, Chris Lister seemed to be increasingly susceptible to illness, and long before it was finished it was obvious that he had cancer. I was struggling with writing the Bonington biography and my own awful emotional state. Yet Chris, in the last stages of his illness, seemed to be as concerned for me as I was for him. In late August we spent a memorable evening together, reliving the good times we had shared (and some of the worst). He told me he wanted to leave me his large collection of climbing books. Through tears, I told him how much his friendship had meant to me and he told me that after his death he wanted his ashes divided amongst his closest friends and scattered somewhere that would always remind us of him.

I suggested a good place would be the ashtray next to the pool table in the pub near Yorkshire Television, where we used to play ferociously competitive games when we were editing both the Destivelle and Sepu Kangri programmes. This made him smile. Then I had a much better idea.

'I suppose it's got to be on the cliffs overlooking the Old Man of Hoy, but it's a bloody long way to go.'

His face lit up. 'That's the place.'

Two weeks later Chris died and a few days after the funeral I was given a small box containing a packet of ashes. I had brought them up to Hoy, well wrapped in sealed poly bags, in the bottom of a pannier.

Now, almost a year after Chris's funeral, I walked up the hill behind the youth hostel on my way over to the Old Man, my brain whirling with memories; of Chris, of Catherine and Erik, of Paul Nunn, my oldest and greatest friend who had been with me on the Old Man in 1983 and on so many other memorable expeditions until, with another friend, Geoff Tier, he was killed by a falling sérac in his beloved Karakoram mountains in 1995.

As I strolled along the path towards the Old Man I was increasingly irritated to see that, even on Hoy, the absurd hand of mindless Nanny State had made its mark. Frequent signs directed me along this, the only path to the Old Man, making it clear to me that, yes, I was going to exactly where I intended, while signs to my left, just above an impressive drop, warned me to beware of dangerous cliffs. As opposed to the safe bouncy kind? I thought. Even the path had been dumbed down with steps and stone slabs. Okay, presumably they were there to stop erosion. But here on the Orkneys, with only a minuscule fraction of the traffic seen on the Pennine Way or the Lake District, was it really necessary to spend good money in this way? Gloomily I imagined the day when hand rails and a moving staircase would be installed, and the Old Man outlined in flashing neon lights in case visitors failed to spot it.

My silent rant was broken by a sudden realisation and I burst out laughing. I'd actually managed to leave the little box of ashes in my tent. I could imagine Chris laughing. Well, I would do my duty by him tomorrow. If Mike Banks and his team had only just embarked on the climb, I would certainly be coming this way again. As I neared the cliff top of the Old Man, I saw two little figures standing watching. One was obviously Pat, Mike's wife.

'Excuse me, but I'm looking for an ancient fossil.' I glanced over the edge of the cliff to a tiny figure at the top of the first pitch of the climb. 'Oh, there he is.'

Pat looked aghast, then did a genuine double take 'Oh, Jim, it's you!' She burst out laughing, 'I thought, what a *very* rude man!' She introduced me to her friend, Jean Douglas, and we watched and chatted in the bright sunshine. Far below, Mike, Richard Sykes and Emma Alsford were on the critical second pitch being filmed by HTV programme-maker, John Alcock. I had a real holiday feeling – this was the first time I'd ever enjoyed watching people climbing on the Old Man without being involved.

I decided to do a drawing. This wasn't a flippant decision. Since I had taken early retirement from the University of the West of England in 1993 I had thrown myself into films and writing. At Bristol I had taught Foundation Students in the Faculty of Art and Design and for most of the week I had been involved in teaching and assessing the work of talented and not so talented eighteen-year-olds. When I left, I never thought I would miss it, and I was right, but in the last couple of years I had started drawing again and when I wrote Chris Bonington's biography I illustrated each chapter with a pencil sketch. I knew that eventually I would return to my roots (I studied painting at art college) when my days as a cameraman were over. I had promised myself that I would draw every day on my bike ride. I quickly realised that making New Year's resolutions like this would be doomed to failure, and so far had only done two or three quick line sketches.

I also realised that sooner or later I would be hoist with my own petard. At Bristol, one of my meaner tricks to students who thought they knew it all (i.e. most of them) was to give them a bicycle to draw or, even worse, ask them to draw one from memory. Now a bike is a deceptively subtle subject with its combination of apparently simple geometry and juxtaposition of two large ellipses. But even the slightest error in assessing angles results in a hopelessly unconvincing effort. Memory drawings were invariably hilarious and a frequent source of embarrassment to the owner who would be made painfully aware of how unobservant we all are most of the time. I could hardly get through with doing a long bike ride without rising to the same challenge and I had visions of past students queuing up to buy the book purely in order to revel in my own shortcomings.

From the earliest visit to Hoy I had been fascinated by the sandstone formations of the Old Man and surrounding cliffs. After a couple of hours' futile effort I admitted something that deep down I had always known – compared with drawing, still photography is a very easy option! I looked at the three or four tentative smudgy efforts I'd produced and realised that a long hard road lay ahead of me. But it was a start and, walking back over the cliff-top path to Rackwick Bay, I felt the kind of heightened perception of my surroundings that for many years had only come from climbing and camerawork.

That evening I was invited round to Dorothy and Jack Rendall's for a wee dram. It was an evening of reminiscing and storytelling. Jack could remember virtually every climber who had made their mark on the Old Man – Joe Brown and his daughter Zoë, Tom Patey, Rusty Baillie, Chris Bonington . . . He amused me with a story of a Sheffield climber I knew well, Jack Street, who on a visit to St John's Head with Ed Ward Drummond had taught the locals a game of darts, apparently unknown until his visit, called Twenty to Ten or Tactics – it is still played to this day.

The Rendalls' daughter Lucy was at home. She was a student nurse and in 1980 had the distinction of being the first baby to be born in Rackwick Bay for thirty-two years. The Orcadian poet, George Mackay Brown, had written a celebratory poem on her birthday and the following day Lucy read it into my tape recorder.

Lullabye For Lucy

Let all plants and creatures of the valley now
Unite,
Calling a new
Young one to join the celebration.

Rowan and lamb and waters salt and sweet
Entreat the
New child to the brimming
Dance of the valley,
A pledge and a promise,
Lonely they were long, the creatures of Rackwick, till
Lucy came among them, all brightness and light.

The poem was set to music by Sir Peter Maxwell Davies, who owns a small cottage in Rackwick Bay, and it had its first performance in St Magnus' Cathedral, Kirkwall, conducted by Peter Maxwell Davies himself.

The next morning I set out again for the Old Man, this time remembering the little box. Everyone has their black humour stories of scattering ashes but I wasn't feeling even vaguely funny. Chris had left a bigger hole in my life than I had been prepared to admit. We had been through many trials and tribulations over the years. His death, at only fifty-nine, seemed so terribly cruel and, despite a long succession of successful films under his belt, Chris never appeared to have had the recognition he deserved. I thought of the endless phone calls and meetings that Chris put himself through to get projects off the ground. He had rarely been able to enjoy the actual adventures he had done so much to instigate. The trip to Hoy had been one of the few exceptions and

Rock Queen, as we had called Catherine's documentary, was his last, and probably best, effort.

I reached the cliff top realising that a bank of sea mist was partially blocking the view of the Old Man. It appeared and disappeared – sometimes only a fragment of its crenellated profile was visible. Somehow these partial revelations made it look a lot bigger than normal. I started to descend the well-known path towards the grassy terrace I remembered so well from filming *Rock Queen*. I could almost see Chris's slight figure standing hunched in the wind and rain. I unwrapped the little packet and threw its contents towards the great sandstone stack, muttering my farewells. Across on the Old Man, Mike and Emma were repeating the second pitch for the benefit of the camera. Been there, done that, I thought, and retraced my steps to the cliff top.

6

Across the Top
of Scotland

Early next morning I cycled back to the ferry after saying my goodbyes to Mike and his team. I intended to spend the day in Stromness to sort out my baggage before catching the late afternoon ferry to Scrabster on the mainland. I'd realised that a fair amount of my kit was now superfluous. In particular, I wanted to send home my light down jacket, some books, including, to my regret, the Bruce Chatwin biography, which I had finished, lots of spare clothing and a mobile phone.

This last, I haven't mentioned up to now. It was my daughter Becky who had insisted and I had only taken it on sufferance. The idea of my pannier ringing as I slogged up some grim Scottish glen in the rain seemed incongruous and faintly distasteful. When I had broken my leg in Scotland with Paul Nunn in the winter of 1995, I had managed (with a huge amount of help from Paul) to drag myself down to the road. A mobile phone would undoubtedly have made the job easier, but I know Paul was pleased that we hadn't had to call out the Mountain Rescue. To take a phone on a bicycle ride would, I thought, be an appallingly wimpish thing to do. But, I gave in. Now, after a week, I hadn't even read the instructions. I cadged a cardboard box from a general store in Stromness and ruthlessly packed everything I thought I didn't need, including the phone, wrapped it all up with sticky tape and posted it. The parcel was quite heavy (and expensive) but,

puzzlingly, seemed to make very little difference to the bike, which still weighed a ton.

Before I left Sheffield I had read a book by Richard and Nicholas Crane, describing a bicycle journey *To the Centre of the Earth*: not the one described by Jules Verne obviously, but the point (in Central Asia) furthest from the sea in any direction. This was a truly epic bike ride, from the mouth of the Ganges, through Bangladesh, India and Nepal, over the Himalaya on to the Tibetan Plateau, then across the desert to a point north of Urumchi which they had calculated was the critical spot. The lads travelled quite incredibly lightly – no tent or stove and relying on food bought at the roadside. They had pared down their possessions to a minimum, even drilling holes through spanners to lighten the load. At times it seemed to me to have been a very dangerous gamble, but it paid off. Their daily mileage was far and away higher than mine (but they were in their twenties and ferociously fit). Even so I still felt that I was being woefully self-indulgent with my ponderous load and briefly considered abandoning the tent and relying simply on a Gore-tex bivvy-bag. But this was Scotland, not Tibet and it was the bivvy-bag that was sent home (thank God).

Once I had posted my parcel I was free to spend a few hours in Stromness. I had fallen in love with the place the first time I saw it in 1982. Its narrow main street is paved and only servicing vehicles are allowed. Clusters of tumbledown houses abut the sea wall and, in the centre, the monolithic Stromness Hotel gloomily dominates the scene. It still feels like a small fishing village, I imagine places like St Ives in Cornwall would have looked similar at the turn of the nineteenth century. I pottered around the shops and stores, absentmindedly buying odds and ends, which was stupid, given that I was trying to lighten the load, browsed through the one bookshop, mainly devoted to Orcadia, if that's the word, and, as it was a nice day, bought some bread and cheese, *The Times* and a can of lager and cycled out of town to find a patch of grass and have a picnic.

As the *St Ola* left Stromness and sailed once again past St John's Head and the Old Man, I remembered that on each of the last three occasions I had made the journey I had thought it would be the last. This time I just assumed that I would be back again (which probably means I won't).

So, I thought, as the Orkneys faded away and the Scottish mainland grew larger, that's the first phase out of the way and no more ferry crossings. The next task would be to cycle back to Sheffield. Too big a thought, that. Let's break it into bite-sized pieces and think positive. I had cycled nearly 200 miles, my bum no longer felt as though it had been marinated in chili sauce, and I had the beginnings of a suntan. The only cause for concern was the numbness in my right hand, which was getting worse, not better. I had rung Mike, my old climbing partner and cycling adviser who guessed (with impressive accuracy) that I had trapped the ulna nerve in my elbow. However, he wasn't so helpful with advice as to how I could untrap it. Neither, I was to find out over the coming weeks, was anyone else.

As to the ride ahead, the first real objective was to ride west across the top of Scotland to the village of Durness near Cape Wrath, then turn south and head for Ullapool. It might be noted that I had no intention of riding the twenty miles each way to John O'Groats. I had already travelled a long way further north and east so it seemed a pointless excursion. Also I still had a vague snobbish fear of being seen to be doing the John O'Groats to Land's End ride.

After a night on the rather boring Thurso campsite (I was the only occupant) I rode into the town to find another bike shop. Inexplicably, the repair kit I bought in Lerwick didn't include a puncture outfit and I realised that I had spent the last ten days without one. To my delight, I also found a secondhand bookshop in which I could have easily spent a whole day but confined myself to buying a couple of paperbacks, selected for bulk rather than merit. Then I set off on a ride I had rather dreaded ever since I had dreamed up the whole idea. I had driven the road to Durness twice before and thought it lonely and desolate. It would probably mean riding into the teeth of the wind and the only point of interest I could remember seeing was The Nuclear Power Development Establishment at Dounreay.

It was a cold misty morning and the bright sunshine of the last few days had disappeared. I cycled up a long, easy-angled hill outside Thurso, gaining height and meeting a fine drizzle hanging in the air. I knew I had just passed an easy opt-out point, as there is a railway link between Thurso and Aberdeen, thence to Edinburgh, York and . . . stop it, stop it . . . I eventually settled down into a sort of rhythm but visibility was down to a few hundred yards, which was a pity because I knew I was missing distant views of Ben Loyal and Ben Hope.

After what seemed about thirty miles but was only really eight or nine, the scattered buildings and strange dome of Dounreay appeared on my right. I stopped for a bite of chocolate and a drink, reflecting on the horrible, temporary-looking architecture housing what was supposedly the fuel of the future. A scathing report had revealed nuclear leaks in the plant which, as usual, had been hushed up. I didn't feel any great urge to hang about and was amused and horrified to see a flock of sheep in a field immediately in front of the plant. 'Where sheep may, or may not, safely graze,' I hummed. I re-mounted the bike, which I was beginning to refer to as The Beast, and peddled off into the mist, into the wind and inevitably up a hill.

The rest of the day remains in my memory as a blur of effort. I kept checking my position on a map and was always being disappointed. I hoped to reach Tongue, which would have made a forty-five-mile day, but as the afternoon wore on and the wind increased, bringing with it flurries of rain, my willpower, which on that day hadn't been much to begin with, flagged alarmingly. I reached the attractively named Bettyhill and to my joy found a real tearoom. More to the point, it was open. The owners, a delightful couple from London, had abandoned their teaching jobs to come and live where they wanted. They showed me a photo of the impressive panorama from their house, which I had not seen for rain and effort. 'Would you swap this for suburbia?' As we chatted, three more cyclists arrived. It quickly became obvious that one of them, a retired man, was a real End-to-Ender. He had set out from Land's End in the grim gales and floods the week before I had left Sheffield and had made it as far as Gloucestershire before giving up when he had found himself pedalling hard downhill, into the teeth of a storm and was so soaked that most of the oil had been scoured from the moving parts on his bike. Reluctantly, he had given up and returned home to Redditch for a few days to recuperate before starting again and now was only a day from the finish. His friends took it in turns to pace him, one cycling, and the other driving.

I envied him his support team but couldn't help feeling that the head down, go for it approach didn't lend itself much to appreciating the countryside. A part of me also envied the fact that this time tomorrow he would have finished, whereas I had hardly started. I wondered what it would feel like to have the end in sight. 'What are you looking forward to most?' This was not a difficult question for him. 'My wife's organising a dinner party on Saturday, then I'll be spending a few days sorting out the garden.' It didn't sound much, but I was jealous. Although I didn't know what his wife was like, I briefly contemplated giving him all my life savings just to swap places. Somehow, I didn't think I would be taken up on my offer. They left wishing me luck and using a phrase that was already becoming a bit of a cliché. 'At least it's downhill all the way for you now.' I had already suffered the ludicrously inaccurate consolation several times (even before I left Sheffield) and it vied for popularity with 'How many miles a day do you do?' and 'Did you do much training before you started?' As the trip wore on and the questions became more and more repetitive I found it harder and harder not to respond with a totally unjustifiable tirade of abuse. (It says a lot for my extraordinary self-restraint and unerring good nature that I never did. But then, that's me all over.)

Only a mile or so beyond the tearoom was a rather nice campsite. Full of tea and buns it wasn't a difficult decision to call at the house where the lady who ran it lived. She looked at me with something approaching pity. 'Would three pounds be all right for one night?' As the sites in Thurso and Lerwick had charged over double that, it was another easy decision to make. What's more the general store opposite sold a rather nice Australian red wine, which neatly accounted for the money I had expected to spend. I cooked up yet another mess, loosely based on chicken curry, quaffed the wine and lost myself in my latest paperback. It was a simple life. I snuggled into my sleeping bag, listening to a faint pattering of rain on the tent. It was the same noise I heard in the morning. Warm and dry in my red cocoon, I dozed on and off hoping it would stop. Eventually I could procrastinate no longer and resigned myself to the first real soaking of the trip. But by the time I had made breakfast and packed up my gear it had stopped. This gave me a good excuse for waiting before taking the tent down to let it dry out. This meant another half hour's reading.

Before I left Sheffield, I had made a tentative plan for my brother Phil and his partner Heather to visit me somewhere in Scotland and spend a day or two walking. I had always wanted to do the traverse of An Teallach, one of the very great classic walks in the whole of Britain; this seemed to be a good opportunity. I had phoned him at home in London the evening I arrived at Rackwick Bay. He wasn't in but later as I passed the red phone box outside the hostel, it started ringing. I went inside and picked it up. It was Phil who had called the last number dialled. To my delight, they had already booked a flight to Glasgow and hired a car. We arranged to meet at the Dundonnell Hotel below An

Teallach in four days' time, which meant I was a day or two ahead of the rough schedule I had sketched on the piece of paper I still kept in my wallet. So today and tomorrow would be quite gentle.

I had promised myself a major treat by staying in the Rhiconich Hotel, between Durness and Scourie. Today, one of my ambitions was to camp somewhere near Durness. As the weather was clearing by the minute and even a few watery rays of sun were hinting at better things, I set out feeling far better than the day before. By the time I was freewheeling down the long hill into Tongue (my original objective for yesterday) I was unaccountably happy. For the first time since I had left Sheffield I seemed to have come to terms with just living in the present, absorbing the sight and sounds around me and not feeling that the whole journey was a penance to be got through. (I was also realistic enough to know that this wouldn't last.)

The road to Durness was built on a causeway across the Kyle of Tongue. I stopped for a drink and some chocolate and sheltered from a cold wind. From here the dark flanks of Ben Loyal disappeared into a cloud base, the weather in the mountains was obviously still poor. I had hoped to walk up it – of course, that was what I had allowed an extra day for. Twenty years ago, I thought, I would have just gritted my teeth and set out. But now there didn't seem to be any point. I love hill walking for the views and, if there aren't any, I prefer the valleys. Even so, I was still slightly tempted until, chilled by the wind, I pedalled across the causeway and started climbing a depressingly straight road that led upwards for as far as the eye could see. By the time I reached its crest and enjoyed the long run down the other side, the clouds had almost blown away, though the top of Ben Hope was still hidden. Not that it mattered; my eyes were fixed on the view ahead. I was now turning south along the shore of Loch Eriboll, one of the biggest, most beautiful and remote sea lochs of all. It was breathtakingly lovely and cycling round the single-track, twisting, undulating road almost completely deserted now in the late afternoon, I didn't want it to end. So much so, that when the road turned at the head of the the loch and I started riding in exactly the wrong direction to home, north-east up towards Durness, I started looking for somewhere to camp and almost immediately found a perfect clearing between the road and the loch that had once been used by road-builders. I found a flat spot for the tent and walked to a little bridge across a stream flowing into the loch that ran with ice-cold crystal clear water.

The light on the hills mellowed and about a mile away a clean-cut crag of pale grey gneiss gleamed in the evening sun. It was probably less than fifty metres high. From ingrained habit, I traced several imaginary climbs up its main features. I wondered if anyone had bothered to explore it, for here it was an insignificant feature in a huge landscape. If it could be transported to Derbyshire it would be probably be a well-known, if minor, crag. Put it in the hop fields of the Kent/Sussex border, amongst the little sandstone crags that I had learned to climb on many years ago, and it could have a guidebook all to itself.

The evening light streaming down on the loch glowed ever brighter, the wind had dropped, though the air was chilly. I congratulated myself on my timing. In a month the midges would make life unbearable. I had treated myself to a half-bottle of cheap whisky in Thurso and poured a generous measure, diluting it with water from the stream to an extent that would horrify most Scots. They would be only slight less appalled to see it being supped from a luminous cherry pink thermally insulated mug that keeps liquid warm for ages. The inside was stained with tea and coffee and even after using it for about five years it still tastes of plastic. But I couldn't have been more content if I had been drinking Glenmorangie out of a Waterford crystal tumbler. I sat outside the tent for a while as the light slowly faded, absorbed by the changing tones of sky, mountains and water. Even the odd pang of unrequited love which still had the power to jolt me like a cattle prod, couldn't spoil the evening and eventually I snuggled into my sleeping bag indulging in a ludicrous fantasy that the object of my affections had finally seen the error of her ways and was even now driving up to the north-west to meet me in a slow-motion embrace set against a backdrop of a flaming sunset plunging into the Atlantic . . . For God's sake, Curran, get real. I fell asleep trying to laugh at myself. I had left the tent door slightly open to look at the stars but the next time I opened my eyes it was to broad daylight and sunshine.

It was slightly frustrating to cycle the next few miles in precisely the opposite way to the one I wished to go, but at least today I would be turning the corner and heading south. There was a stiff breeze blowing in my face but I was sustained by the thought that once I reached the big left turn it would be more or less behind me. Slowly, the landmarks I had passed yesterday on the other side of Loch Eriboll slipped away and I rode out over the moor to Durness. From here to Ullapool I would be riding through familiar territory. For years Sheffield climbers, led invariably by Paul Nunn and members of the Alpha Club, had spent the Whit bank holiday up here, normally camped near the little beach at Sheigra. From here they had explored the sea cliffs around Cape Wrath, climbed on the crags of Foinaven, particularly on the great buttress of Dionard, and drunk in the hotels of Kinlochbervie and Rhiconich. Every year's events would be added to an already large fund of stories and the whole area had taken on an almost legendary status. I had never really been a part of the tradition, because when I worked in Bristol I only had the Whit Monday off, but on the rare occasions I had made it, I had become as hooked as anyone else. After Paul's death in the Karakoram in 1995 some of us still went up there, particularly Hilary, Paul's widow, but the driving force was gone and it had become a place of memories. Also, truth to tell, we were all getting a bit long in the tooth for serious climbing.

Once out of Durness and past the point where a short ferry

takes you out to the Cape Wrath peninsula, I rode happily up towards the Rhiconich Hotel. On my right, the turquoise waters of the Kyle of Durness mingled with wide stretches of yellow sand shimmering in the afternoon sun. All too soon the shoreline receded and I started on what I knew was a long, long uphill stretch. Almost as soon as I started, another cyclist came free-wheeling down in the opposite direction and we stopped for a chat. He was from Liverpool, had only a week's holiday and was travelling light, doing an impressive mileage each day. I had been quite surprised to see so few cyclists around. (Apart from the Land's End to John O'Groats guy and a couple on the ferry I couldn't remember anyone else at all.) And it was nice to talk to someone. Maybe I was even getting a lot more confident about the whole biking culture. At least I wasn't interrogated about gears or sprockets. When we parted, however, I was conscious of his gaze as I laboured uphill, and was determined to keep a reasonable pace until he was out of sight, which took an inordinately long time. Ahead, the road wound inexorably upward. A large touring coach rumbled past and disappeared round a bend, re-emerging as a tiny object miles up the road and staying in sight for ages as it ground up to the top of the hill. God, it was a long way.

As I pedalled slowly upwards I distracted myself by comparing my self-imposed journey with a strange TV series called *Castaway* that had fascinated me before I set out and was being enacted not so far away. Thirty random people had been selected to spend a year on Taransay, a tiny Hebridean island. The BBC had chosen them from hundreds of applicants with the aid of a psychologist and a series of Outward-Bound-style tests to assess suitability, so they weren't that random. They weren't really castaways either, for each member could bring a large box of possessions, and specialised dwellings were being built for them. They also had mail and emergency communication with the outside world (I found out in a later programme, that they also had a thriving smuggling trade as well.) What had amazed me was how so many of the group were so intolerant and often extremely unpleasant to each other. It was like the worst expedition you could ever imagine going on, though, of course, it made for good viewing figures, presumably the point of the whole exercise. It was so different from normal life that stress and strain quickly began to show in front of the camera. I wondered if I would have found it harder or easier to cope, given the amount of time I had spent on trips in confined groups over the years.

My reverie was interrupted by my arrival at the top and I celebrated with a drink and a rest. Another cyclist rode past (two in one day!) and checked that I was okay – a nice gesture and one I made a mental note to make myself in future. Then it was time for the long, exhilarating descent to creature comforts. The Rhiconich Hotel is run by a Sheffield husband and wife team, Ray and Helen Fish. Like the couple from Bettyhill they had taken a big gamble to change their lives. I had only stayed in the hotel once, but had often spent evenings in the bar, on the walls of which hung photos of Dionard Buttress and the nearby sea stack Am Buachaille. They were the same photos that hung in Hilary Nunn's hallway. My one previous night in the Rhiconich was with Catherine and Erik after making the Hoy film, when we had spent two days driving round the west coast on our way back to Edinburgh airport. Then the hotel bill had been paid by Northern Films and this time it was my own money. But I felt I had earned a treat.

I treated myself to a long wallow in a bath as hot as I could bear, and then had an awesomely huge steak and chips in the restaurant, before ending the evening watching TV from the splendour of my double bed. Earlier, I had rung an old friend in Bristol and left a message. Now the phone rang and Carole's incredulous voice asked me what the hell I was up to. When I told her, she was unimpressed. 'This time, Curran,' she announced imperiously, 'You've really lost the plot.' No amount of explaining on my part could convince her that I had not taken leave of my senses. Eventually, in a rather sniffy way, she conceded that it might not be quite as barmy as climbing on K2 or filming on the Old Man of Hoy.

'Oh well, I suppose at least it's downhill all the way.'

SUILVEN FROM LOCHINVER

7

Lord of the Fly

The Rhiconich Hotel was another opportunity for lightening my load. After breakfast I rummaged through my panniers, trying to cut out anything superfluous. Two of the Old Spice Girls, Hilary Nunn and Pam Beech, had hired a cottage near Sheigra, for the spring bank holiday and Hilary always popped in to visit Ray and Helen, so I left a parcel for her to collect. Naturally, despite its weight, it didn't seem to make any difference to the Beast.

It was another lovely day, but windy. This time it seemed to be coming from the south-east. At the village of Scourie, my midday break, I shivered in the sunshine, then turned directly into the wind and commenced the worst few hours of the ride so far. I was aiming for the new bridge at Kylesku. Every revolution of the pedals seemed to demand a separate effort of will and on one long uphill stretch the road ran between two embankments that funnelled the gale. In the lowest of the granny gears I could hardly make headway and I began to experience horrible flashes of self-doubt and self-pity. Could I face battling all the way down the country against the prevailing wind? When the elegant modern single-span bridge came into sight, I had had enough. But there was no sign of anywhere to camp, with or without permission and on the other side of the bridge, the road once again rose sharply up a narrow valley. At my lowest ebb, I noticed a providential sign directing me up a steep track to bunkhouse accommodation. Thank you, God.

Actually, given that it had a sitting room (with books and TV), a dining room and kitchen, as well as several bedrooms, it seemed that 'bunkhouse' was an unnecessarily austere description. It was remarkably cheap and the only other occupants were a young German couple touring the Highlands. They insisted, curiously, on only communicating in hushed whispers when in my presence which made me distinctly uneasy, though they were only trying to be polite. Unless, of course, they were spies, which seemed unlikely.

The last few days had been quite tiring but I was looking forward to the next, as I would be cycling past Quinag, Suilven, Stac Polly and Ben Mor Coigach on my way to Ullapool. Here I planned a rest day, as Phil and Heather wouldn't arrive until the day after. I got up early, before the whispering started, and managed to leave soon after eight, which for me was a bit of a triumph. The wind had dropped and soon I began to get excited as the long crenellated ridge of Quinag appeared and I started looking out for Suilven. Though not even a Munro, Suilven's majestic form, as it rises from the moorland, never falls to impress me. I had wanted to climb it for years, but hadn't got round to it until 1997. Then, while giving a couple of lectures in Aviemore and Inverness, I grabbed the chance of doing both Stac Polly and Suilven between venues. Suilven from Lochinver had been a memorable day: starting at first light in order to get back to the car by early afternoon and driving hell-for-leather to the lecture in Aviemore. Two months later, while filming for a BBC programme called *Tracks*, I had climbed Suilven again this time from Inverkirkaig. There is something indefinable about its rounded twin summits and interconnecting ridge that fires my imagination. Though it can't compare with Ushba in the Caucasus, or Nanda Devi in the Indian Himalaya which are probably the best-known and most spectacular twin-summitted peaks in the world, little Suilven, by its very isolation in the middle of a great moorland setting, has grandeur out of all proportion to its size.

Before I got there I arrived at the junction with the main A837 to Inverness and suffered what would prove to be the first of many attacks of signpost rage. This phenomenon, which really only affects cyclists and walkers, is where you pass a signpost informing you that your destination is, say, fifteen miles distant, then a mile or so later, another one which might say either exactly the same thing or, possibly, that it is now seventeen miles away. Now, I have never understood things like the International Date Line where time travel appears to be possible, or the theory of relativity with the Daliesque light-bending and curved space, but presumably people who erect road signs do. Either that or they simply can't be arsed to remember what the last one they put up ten minutes ago actually said. It is easy to feel like the traveller on a walking tour in Ireland who, having been told several times during a long day that he was only twenty miles from his objective, wearily observed, 'Thank God I'm holding my own.' This time, having passed two contradictory signs, and restrained an impulse to dismount and head-butt the second one, I was distracted by the appearance of Suilven, and for the next few miles became a danger to traffic as I couldn't take my eyes off it. My happiness was complete as a roadside café materialised just when I wanted it. There were tables and sunshades outside and a cup of tea and a bacon sandwich seemed to be in order. I regret to say that my pleasure was not enhanced by the arrival of a Glaswegian couple. The wife was seriously overweight. (I know, I know, I shouldn't say things like that – look who's talking, etc., etc., but she was.) The man, however, was just grotesque, at least thirty stone and quite possibly a lot more. I could have felt quite sorry for him, except that it must have been his choice to wear a too-small T-shirt and baggy shorts. The former revealed a less than alluring acreage of stomach whose pendulous folds hung over the latter, which sadly were not quite long enough and revealed lily white legs ravaged by eczema, at which he scratched incessantly. As he consumed a vast plate of double sausage and chips and bread and butter, he displayed all this for my benefit, while I tried not to choke on my bacon butty and thought of Ethiopia and Oxfam.

Before I left, I got into conversation with the café owner – another Londoner. Where were all the locals? In London, I supposed, running New Labour or something. I pointed out, without much originality, that it was a lovely day. He agreed, but observed gloomily that it had been like this the previous year until just about the same day, from whence it had rained until the autumn. He thought the same thing might happen again. 'Nonsense my man!' I wanted to exclaim heartily, patting him reassuringly on the back, 'This is set for weeks.' But I knew full well it wasn't. Even so, I couldn't have known how accurate his prophecy was to be.

In the afternoon the view of Suilven was replaced by glimpses of Stac Polly, Am Fhidlear and, away in the distance, the unmistakable outline of my next objective, An Teallach. Before I reached Ullapool, I rode by the side of the lovely little Ardmair Bay which, with its perfect crescent sweep, leads the eye back to Ben Mor Coigach. One more steep hill. Then it was down into the fleshpots of Ullapool.

There is no getting away from the fact that the pretty little town on the edge of Loch Broom, is dangerously near to being twee. The waterfront shops are, in the main, devoted to Highland woollens, Highland crafts and Highland postcards of Highland castles. Even so, I have always found it a romantic spot. The ferry to Stornaway in the Hebrides leaves from here and the point is often visited by Russian trawlers. This time a Russian cruise ship was docked in the middle of the loch. I found it hard to imagine hordes of the Moscow Mafia spending their ill-gotten roubles on little model bagpipes, tartan golfing trousers and tins of shortbread, but you never know.

I pedalled into town looking forward to a short break and found a campsite out on the lochside. Unlike every previous one, there were actually people on it, some in tents, but mainly in caravans. It made a change. As I was staying two nights I thought I'd get really well organised and spent a tedious hour or so reducing the tent and my belongings to a state of comfortable squalor. Why is it that I employ a cleaner once a fortnight and spend most of the day before she comes, attempting to create order out of chaos? On her arrival she only has to cast her eyes around the living room and everything falls meekly into place. It is a trick I don't understand, like the tricks of changing duvet covers and ironing shirts. There must be a tidying up gene that I lack. I can't even blame it on my sex, for I know many men who are perfectly at ease with a Hoover or a mop and bucket. But not me.

I slept well and spent the next morning lying outside the tent on my Thermorest reading the *Sunday Times*. Above me, high swirling clouds moved in – the forerunners of bad weather? However, it stayed sunny. My only worry was that perhaps I should have pressed on and grabbed the traverse of An Teallach while I could, but this seemed very unfair on Phil and Heather who were coming so far to meet me.

If the weather was breaking down, it was doing it very slowly – there might still be time. The day passed in a warm stupor, dozing, reading, dozing again, walking into town, and inevitably finding a bookshop, where I bought two John Irving paperbacks, *A Prayer for Owen Meany* and *The Ciderhouse Rules*. Enough to see me into England I hoped.

I also spent some time looking at the map. On my large-scale one I had done quite well – from Thurso to Ullapool seemed to be a reasonably significant chunk. But on a map of Scotland, I wasn't making much headway. Still a good way north of where I had caught the ferry in Aberdeen. On the little map on the cover, showing the whole of England and Scotland, I had hardly started.

Monday dawned dull. It wasn't raining but it was obvious that the fine spell was coming to an end. I packed up and left Ullapool feeling tired and jaded. Not really surprising this, for I had found on expeditions that rest days often leave you feeling worse than before. My mood wasn't helped as I cycled a long straight road flanked by pine trees. It took a few minutes for the penny to drop, and then I remembered that as a child an unintentionally sinister poster in the London Underground had terrified me. It was a simple illustration of two small children holding hands and walking away down a narrow road through a dark pine forest. The caption read 'Children's Shoes Have Far To Go', an advertisement for Start-Rite shoes, if I remember correctly. It could reduce me to helpless tears and my mother later told me that if she spotted one before I did she would walk me to the other end of the platform to avoid the embarrassment of my pathetic sobbing and the stares of fellow travellers. It had obviously left a permanent mark and half a century later the feeling, if not the tears, returned.

The road steepened and became a GOAP (get off and push). I reached a lay-by at the famous Falls of Measach where there was a tea shack with a fine view back down the loch to Ullapool. A German coach party arrived with the most beautiful Scottish lass as their guide. Dozens of aged overweight couples tottered off to view the waterfall, accompanied, I was disappointed to note, by the girl with whom I had already decided to spend the rest of my days. On her return, she got straight on to the coach and it drove off. At least this time my broken heart recovered in five minutes.

Above the falls, I left the main road to Inverness and turned right onto the Road of Destitution (built during the 1851 potato famine), still climbing gradually and heading over bleak moorland towards An Teallach, now quite large on the skyline. Although it was cloud-free I was not optimistic as a chill wind blew from the west. Having pedalled uphill for most of the morning, I was relieved to find the road levelling out, then plunging in a long and glorious freewheel. It went on and on as all the energy I had stored up on the uphill side was released (I'm not sure if it is scientifically correct, but that's the way it felt). The only fly in the ointment was the one that collided with my left eye at a combined speed of about 70 miles an hour. It almost knocked my head off and I freewheeled the last couple of miles with tears streaking my cheek as I attempted to remove bits of legs, body and wings from all corners of my face.

When the road flattened out, I freewheeled into a large lay-by, aiming to stop and lean the bike against a litter bin. More or less one-eyed, I ground to a halt and somehow managed to miss the bin. Still with my feet trapped in the pedal clips, I gently toppled over and crashed to the ground. Luckily there was no one around to witness this embarrassing débâcle and, wiping away tears and some more lumps of fly, I checked out the Beast before cycling the last few miles to the Dundonnell Hotel. It looked far too expensive to welcome a dishevelled cyclist but I asked at Reception if my brother had arrived, which he hadn't. Then I went to the bar and ordered a pint before going to the gents, where, glancing in the mirror, I realised why both the receptionist and the barman had recoiled in horror. My eye was bloodshot and running, big frag-ments of fly were still lodged in various crannies, my jacket was crumpled and muddy with dead leaves stuck to it from the litter bin episode, and I was still wearing my cycle helmet which, at the best of times, made me look like an elderly alien. If they thought I looked in a bad way, I told myself, they should have seen the fly. All the same, I made a hasty attempt to clean up before returning to the bar to finish my pint.

I really didn't want to stay in the hotel, so I cycled on a mile or so until I came upon a collection of houses which included another bunkhouse. It was immaculately clean and nobody was staying there, so I checked in before returning to wait for Phil and Heather's arrival and conducted them down the road to the hotel. Then I succumbed to a long attack of verbal diarrhoea, hardly surprising, for they were the first friends that I had met since Mike Banks, which seemed a long time ago.

A husband and wife team from Edinburgh arrived and we got talking. They were both keen walkers and cyclists and I told them my plans, such as they were. They came up with a brilliant suggestion. I had been quietly worrying about the ride through central Scotland, particularly dealing with the heavy traffic around Edinburgh and Glasgow. They suggested that from Glencoe, I ride down to Oban, then down to the Kintyre peninsula and catch the small ferry, which only runs in summer, across to the Isle of Arran. From there, I could cycle round the island to the main ferry back to Ardrossan and thus cut out the Glasgow/Edinburgh section completely. It wouldn't save many miles, but it would be a far more attractive route. I would then go down to Dumfries, across to Gretna Green and into England. It was a neat idea with the added attraction that from Oban it would all be new ground for me. However, it was seriously jumping the gun to even think that far ahead.

I went to sleep that night with some misgivings. The traverse of An Teallach (pronounced, incidentally, An Shellac) is one of the most serious Highland scrambles and there have been several deaths on its sandstone ridges. I was slightly worried about taking Phil and Heather on it in anything less than perfect weather. Wait and see, I told myself as I went to sleep. To my surprise the day dawned bright but with clouds building up. We got away early, after a suitably large breakfast. I allowed myself to be driven the three or four miles to the start of the walk as it was back along the road I had already cycled and didn't seem to contravene any rules I'd laid down for myself.

We set off. Heather, fit and long-legged soon striding ahead of me. Phil stayed with me and we chatted our way along the first three miles of very gentle uphill. I had decided that it would be best to start from the far end of the ridge, as it would be safer ascending the difficult bits, and we would also be doing this earlier in the day. When we reached an ill-defined col the path split; the main one descending into the Great North-West Wilderness where a path led off to Shenavall and from there across to the Fisherfield Forest, Carnmore and Fionn Loch. Our rough path turned right, leading on to Sail Liath, the first summit along the ridge. Soon any semblance of path ran out and the hillside degenerated into a pile of loose rocks up which we picked our separate paths. Another couple came in sight and we all stumbled around, convinced that everyone else had found an easier way.

As we reached our first minor summit the black clouds that had been amassing in the west all day at last swept over us. It started raining and the wind picked up. We stopped for a drink and some chocolate. Rivulets of water ran down my Gore-tex jacket. The rest of the ridge was now hidden in black cloud. It rained harder and got noticeably colder. 'Oh sod it!' It was pointless to continue and probably irresponsible as well, for Heather had never attempted anything as serious as I knew this would certainly become. The other couple made the same decision at the same moment and we all retraced our individual footsteps back to the main path. Perversely, as we walked back to the car, it actually stopped raining and the ridge momentarily appeared through torn clouds. But I am sure we had made the right decision. As Don Whillans used to say: 'The mountain will still be 'ere next year. The trick is to make sure you are as well.'

RAIN OVER THE TRIPLE BUTTRESSES OF COIRE MHIC FHEARCHA

8

Fionn Buttress

Phil and Heather decided to drive to Gairloch, so it was another luxury day for me because they had offered to take my panniers with them. But I spent most of it wondering again why lightening the load seemed to make so little difference. Maybe it is simply that the bicycle is such an efficient form of transport. On foot, to be relieved of your rucksack makes a colossal difference, particularly towards the end of a long day, when you can actually imagine yourself levitating.

Between Gruinard Bay and Loch Ewe, I started glancing to my left, for I knew that I was as close as I would get on this trip to one of the most remote and splendid of Scottish crags, Carnmore, overlooking Fionn Loch. It was coming here by mountain bike with Terry Gifford that was the beginning of my re-acquaintance with the bicycle back in 1992. I wrote about our climb on Fionn Buttress in *High* magazine while the memories of that wonderful visit were still sharp, and Terry's poem was intercut with the article:

> Surrounded by mountains and high above the rushing river, I'm completely out of control, utterly useless, a gibbering wreck. Help, press the panic button. Full Red Alert – I'm definitely going to fall off – not I'm not – Oh, yes you are – get a grip – concentrate – you're going to kill yourself . . .

It was, in my defence, my first cycle ride in over 30 years, and this was on an overloaded mountain bike wearing a heavy rucksack

and big boots. Luckily for me, after only three miles of uncon-
trolled panic, contrasted with fits of giggles and what felt like a
pile driver up my nether regions, the deer fence of the Letterewe
Estate abruptly foiled further progress/damage. 'No bicycles
whatsoever' proclaimed the sign on the gate, amongst a long list of
other prohibitions. Relieved, I slung the bike in a gorse bush next
to Terry Gifford's, who locked them up. Eight miles of walking
beckoned. I doubted that we would ever see the bikes again and I
wasn't sure if I was sorry or not.

It had been Terry's idea for Whit weekend. 'Fionn Buttress,' he
had enthused. 'Bike in, do the route, bike out, completely painless
and the best VS in Scotland.' I agreed to go, with the proviso that
we had a poetry embargo on the whole weekend. 'No rhyming
couplets,' I insisted, before remembering that none of Terry's
poems rhymed anyway.

> Fionn freedom
> comes from a journey not a fight
> steady patience
> savouring acceptance
> of the ever-wet, the elusive distance,
> the commitments of flesh to place:
>
> Wester Ross
> Poolewe
> Carnmore Crag
> Fionn Buttress
>
> bikes, boots
> big sacks
> plasters
> bothy, tents

So it was that two footsore and weary old men reached the

halfway point and breasted the gentle rise that concealed the longed-for view of Fionn Loch and Carnmore Crag. I had been here once before many years ago, and was suitably shamefaced when Terry pointed out that we had been staring at our objective for the last hour or so.

As we slowly gained the end of Loch Fionn, Carnmore Crag took the ferocious aspect familiar from many photos, with its huge roof of Gob and the Cenotaph-like walls of Carnmore Corner high above. On the left side of the crag Fionn Buttress looked long above and wonderful, nine pitches of sustained and intricate 4b/4c climbing. What more could we ask for? Not having blisters, burrowing sheep ticks and bloody great rucksacks sprang instantly to mind as we plodded over the causeway and round to the bothy below the crag, passing several more notices reminding us that we were in the wilderness area.

It was indeed a wilderness. Surrounding Carnmore Lodge were rusting oil drums and wheelbarrows, sheets of corrugated iron, cement bags and broken barbed-wire fences. They contrasted incongruously with orders not to camp and respect the country-side. Sighing yet again at man's seemingly complete inability to recognise his own folly, we settled down to a late afternoon of eating, brewing and crag watching. The sun sank slowly, lighting the buttresses of Ben Lair and the endless vistas of more mountains and lochs stretching away to the west . . .

In late May we were spared the ravages of midges (though not the aforementioned sheep ticks) and the necessity of an early start. Carnmore faces south-west and doesn't get the sun until mid-morning, which then stays on it until late in the evening. So we actually had to restrain ourselves from leaving the bothy until 10.30, and walk gently up to the narrow path skirting the great sweep of slabs and overhangs above. We deliberately decided to take it very slowly, savouring every move of each pitch.

I had waited twenty years for this route and I started up the first pitch. It wasn't particularly distinguished and the next, which was Terry's, was even less so. It led to the foot of a short pedestal leaning against an immaculate slab of pale grey gneiss (that's granite to you and me). The pitch could have been specially designed to the specifications of a fully paid-up member of the Byron Slab Climbing Club (BSCC), a title originally coined by Steve Bancroft to describe that august body of elderly and obese gentlemen who frequent the hostelry of that name in Sheffield, and who all share the common ability to perform more than adequately on rock the right side of vertical, as they do the opposite when on the wrong side. The slab in front of me was supplied with perfect and unexpected letterbox-shaped slots that led to a final steepening and a few committing moves to the sanctuary of a good ledge and belay.

Ego suitably boosted, I dismissively waved Terry through to cope with the next pitch, which led to the crux. He took his time, not, I soon came to realise, because he was battling with the desire to knock off a couple of stanzas before lunch, but because it was wet, hard and badly protected.

> limestone letterboxes
> reward a blind reach,
> Etive edges
> enlighten a long stare,
> wet pocket
> dry pocket
> wet pocket
> slap and step
> The Overhang

Thankfully the crux, which now loomed above, looked dry and well protected. We took stock and sorted out the gear. Now Terry is methodical and racks his gear in order of size, and function. I suppose all climbers do nowadays. It gave him the look of a man in complete control. That is to say, it would have, were it not for the fact that such meticulous attention to detail was offset by his attire, which consisted mainly of an ancient helmet and a similarly vintage pair of underpants, Terry, having left his shorts in the bothy. Consequently by the end of a long day the negative image of his harness was stencilled around his upper legs, set off by a large acreage of rather fetching lobster pink sunburn. A sight of sore thighs, you might say.

Unable to put off the moment any longer and encouraged by Terry's supportive presence, I left the belay and sidled unobtrusively across to the big overhangs hoping they wouldn't notice me. The route sneaks through at the narrowest point, which seemed to bristle with big juggy flakes. Surely even a member of the BSCC could manage it? Well, yes and no. After a modicum of nervous teetering and some complex jugglements of rope and runners, I realised that 'if the deed were to be done 'twere best done quickly.' Feet up high, undercut jam and reach the first flake, great, now a big heave, get your feet up higher – reach with your right – shit, it isn't a jug – too late now – pinch it and get your right foot up – judder, shake, done it, quick get a runner in. 'Piece of piss actually.' Out came the ritual cliché.

After a few more easy moves up and round a little corner, I reached the perfect post-crux belay, braced on bombproof large nuts and a Friend, while perched on a sloping slab and looking down into a quite respectable void. Terry made short work of it and then set off on what appeared to be a mind-blowing traverse. It was inexplicably ungraded, given its wild situation. Luckily it wasn't desperate but it did involve two long steps across and down, a classic second's nightmare. Thankfully, Terry put on runners after, as well as before, the bad bits so that I didn't burst into tears once.

'You have to want it'

this move
this route
this place

traverse the wilderness
step across the wild space
on gneiss holds
to the soaring alternatives:
slab, wall, arête
and somewhere a 'step left'

I joined him perched on the very edge of the buttress. Above were a vertical groove and some very grown-up looking country indeed. 'I thought we'd done the hard bits.' Nervous and slightly weary, I found leaving the ledge both awkward and strenuous. Then, perhaps as a result of the heat, euphoria and fright, I failed to make sense of the route description and went very wrong indeed.

Lured by a beautiful, grey slab I climbed to its tapering crest and came hard up against a vertical wall topped by an overhang. I should have hand-traversed left about thirty feet below. To my right was a huge nest, surely belonging to a pterodactyl? Luckily, the owner wasn't at home. Straight up was out of the question, which left the vertical wall and arête to my left. Gulp. A small Friend in a horizontal break gave me a bit of Dutch courage and I hauled up onto the first flat holds, stood up and just managed to reach the arête with my left hand.

Now, I am forty-nine going on fifty and it crossed my mind quite forcibly that heel-hooking with my left foot was an absurd and poseurish thing to do at my age, like going to an acid house party, wearing an earring, or trying to grow a ponytail, but if I didn't do something p.d.q. I would be off, and I am certainly far too old to entertain even the thought of a leader fall. I wasn't entirely convinced that heel-hooking wouldn't simply make airtime a certainty but it was all I could think of doing. 'Watch the ropes,' I squeaked down to Terry, by now so far below that it didn't much matter what he did. By pressing with my right hand, piano-playing with my left up the arête and pawing ineffectually round the corner with my heel, calf and anything else, I lurched upwards and at full stretch grabbed a superb incut slot with my right hand. Dry-mouthed with terror, I peeped round the arête. Joy of joys, big holds appeared only just out of reach. Rather neatly, I thought, but from Terry's vantage point in blind panic, I tiptoed across a steep lichenous slab and grabbed the jugs. As I did so a rope jammed solid. Christ, give us a break – I wrenched furiously, to no avail. At full reach I could just place a comforting Friend 3, clip the other rope and tension back down. Ironically, the rope had jammed in the life-saving incut slot. Relief swept over me as I freed it and hauled back to big holds, ledges, easy angles and bombproof belays.

Terry came up quickly, cold and stiff from his windy vigil below. I was pleased he slowed down for the last bit, but maybe he was just trying to please me. Poets can sometimes be like that. As all his other pitches had been ungraded and mildly desperate, we hoped that the next pitch, given 4b, would be much easier and so it was, apart from a curious pull-up on colossal blocks apparently completely detached, around which Terry threaded slings, presumably to act as extra ballast to his not exactly petite self should he and the blocks part company. After that, a short, juggy wall, then my turn again.

The last pitch was up really easy ground: slabs, a little traverse, a last wall and suddenly – hey, no more crag. Bemused, I pulled over into a horizontal world, full of great bubbling joy at the best route of its grade I'd ever done. In the cloudless late afternoon, Terry emerged rapturous. I could have forgiven him if he had addressed me in blank verse in Latin at that moment, but even he was lost for words. (That didn't last long.)

rising wind
drooping sun
white slab
rising wall
flat grass, suddenly
and the best walk off in the world
complete with drinking drip

the best dram in the world
is backs to the bothy wall now
feet in mud, bums on 'sacks
sun setting sideways
and Fionn Loch winking back

first light through the tent skin
snipe drumming and drumming
greenshank shrilling up from the bog

and the walk out
past sparkling wind-scoured water
over the narrow causeway

cairned at each end by cement
and a metal sign declaring:

No camping
No litter
No fire anywhere

Walkers keep to the footpaths
No mountain bikes
No fishing
No vehicles except on estate business

Please help us preserve
This precious wilderness

To put icing on the cake, the way down was simplicity itself. We skirted the base of the crag to our 'sacks and watched two tiny figures high above us whose voices we had occasionally heard during the day. They were actually doing the pitch after the traverse the right way. But now it didn't matter, nothing mattered. In a trance I strolled down to the bothy lost in my dreams. Blisters, sheep ticks and big rucksacks, the rest of my life, could all wait until tomorrow.

Nine years had passed, but Fionn Buttress still holds its own in my memory as one of the best days I have had anywhere. At its grade, Very Severe, it has the position and character of much harder climbs. I wondered when, or if, I would ever return, for there were still other wonderful routes to do. Now I freewheeled down the wet road past Inverewe Gardens, famous for their palm trees and tropical plants that flourish in the sheltered recess of Loch Ewe and are warmed by the Gulf Stream. Swathes of rain dripped across the landscape, but it cheered up a bit at the tiny village of Poolewe and I stopped at a store for food and drink. I found a bench to sit on. Terry and I had left the car here last time and I briefly wished that I could simply put the Beast onto a bike-carrying frame and get a lift home. This was rather an ominous thought, for I was hoping to meet Terry in Glencoe in about a week's time and I feared that the temptation might be too strong. Once again, I tried to put the negative thoughts out of my mind and narrowed my horizons to the here and now.

After an evening with Phil and Heather, I left Gairloch early, stopping only to buy a can of Lucozade and a bar of chocolate. Though I thought I was in for a nice gentle ride I had forgotten a big hill immediately outside the town, before the flat road up the lochside to Kinlochewe. As I neared the top Phil and Heather drove past and waved. Just as they went out of sight, I heard a soft 'psssht' and thought for a stupid moment that the Lucozade had exploded. Jarring bumps from the back wheel quickly enlightened me. Bugger it, a puncture. Ah well, it had to happen sooner or later. At least this had occurred immediately opposite a rest area with wooden benches and trestle seats and a lovely view that, just at that moment, l wasn't particularly concerned with. I pushed the Beast over to a bench and systematically removed the panniers, found the tool kit and puncture outfit. I turned the bike upside down, had a brief oily but successful encounter with the chain, the back wheel and the derailleur gears, then, rather to my surprise, I managed to remove the tyre and the inner tube. A cyclist passed.

'Okay, mate?'

'No problem,' I lied, pretending to be cheerful and furtively reading the instructions for a job I hadn't done in almost forty years. I found the puncture and patched it quite easily, then pumped some air into the tyre to check it had worked. Then I started to get the tube and tyre back onto the wheel. I just couldn't remember the trick with the tyre levers and wrestled unsuccessfully for what seemed like hours. It started raining – hard. My temper was not improved by the arrival of a large Mercedes with German registration, driven by a stunning-looking woman who pulled up, laughed at me and drove off, narrowly avoiding a rock being thrown at her receding bodywork (of the car, naturally). At last the tyre flipped onto the wheel, which I eventually managed to slot back onto the frame and re-engage the chain and gears. I pumped it up hard and rode around the lay-by feeling smug, if damp. Then I hooked up the panniers and celebrated with a drink and some chocolate. As I chewed the chocolate, I glanced at the Beast out of the comer of my eye and did a double take. The back wheel was as flat as a pancake. Fuck.

There was no point in losing my temper and so, fighting a strong desire to throw the Beast into the lochan below, I performed the same ritual once again, this time finding another puncture quite close to the first. I couldn't understand how I'd managed to miss it and checked inside the tyre for anything sharp that might still be there. Eventually, I re-assembled everything, tested it as before, and set off with a huge sigh of relief.

I had just started freewheeling down towards Loch Maree when I felt a strange bumping. Looking down I saw, to my horror, the back tyre was swelling like a boa-constrictor that had swallowed a pig. I ground to a halt, cursing steadily and eloquently. A section of the tyre about six inches long was coming apart and the inner tube was protruding like a hernia, I had to stop by the side of the road and yet again do the dreaded business. When I got the tyre off this time I regret to say I hurled it as far as I could into the lochan where it made a pathetic splash and disappeared. Then I fitted the spare I had providentially decided was worth carrying (I had nearly sent it home) and at last got under way, by now soaked and fed up to the back teeth. The rain was lashing down but, amazingly the wind was behind me and when I reached the slopes of Loch Maree I could actually bomb along quite quickly, which warmed me up a bit. Slioch, on the north side of the loch, was shrouded in cloud and driving rain.

When I arrived in Kinlochewe I stopped at the hotel which had bunkhouse accommodation attached. To my surprise, Phil and Heather had booked into the hotel and they immediately received a detailed and explicit account of my misfortunes from the moment they had driven past. I think they were quite awestruck by my imaginative use of the English language (which they both teach to overseas students, minus, presumably, the obscenities). Phil couldn't stop laughing, which I suppose is a brother's prerogative. The good weather had definitely broken and the forecast was for more of the same: 'scattered showers, heavy at times', to use the time-honoured phrase. 'Pissing down over the mountains' was what it really meant. Phil and Heather left for Glasgow in the morning. As they departed, I couldn't swear it, but I thought I heard Phil say something about it all being downhill from here.

For my part, I turned onto the A896 to Torridon. I had a sneaky little ambition to attempt a solo climb on the Triple Buttress of Coire Mhic Fhearchair, the wonderful sandstone ramparts on the north-west flanks of the Ben Eighe. I had completed the traverse of its sister peak Liathach three or four years earlier, another classic scrambling sort of ridge walk. Ben Eighe itself is not so interesting but I was confident that I could climb a long route of Very Difficult standard on its major crag. I cycled up to the little car park between the two mountains and set out, trying not to feel too optimistic, carrying only my rock boots, chalk bag and a Gore-tex jacket. For the first time I worried slightly about the security of the Beast and the panniers. It would be very easy to steal from a car park and locking it to a litter bin was little more than a gesture.

It seemed further than I remembered and I certainly didn't feel particularly dynamic. I remembered years and years ago thinking that cycling and walking were very different ways of hurting your body. Somehow, I couldn't get into a comfortable walking stride and the path up to the col and round to the lochan below Coire Mhic Fhearchair seemed to take a lot longer than I expected. As I caught my first sight of the great buttresses it started raining, at first little spots that splashed onto the still waters of the lochan, then, as a grey cloud swept across the cliffs, it fell in earnest. I put my jacket on and stared gloomily across the water. The buttress gleamed with a silvery sheen, and climbing was obviously out of the question. There was little point in hanging around, so I retraced my steps.

By the time I had retrieved the Beast and set off down the road to Torridon it had stopped raining but I felt both tired and depressed. There was a little field at Torridon in which I had camped years ago with my elder daughter, Gemma. Then it had been infested with midges and to my horror it still was. Midge City we had called it at the time and there was no reason to change the name. I had thought that by trying to ride through Scotland before the end of May I would escape the full horror of these little beasties, but it was not to be. I could almost hear them passing the message around: 'Hey, do you remember that bloke who came here once with his daughter? Well, you won't believe this, but he's back again and, guess what! he's even fatter and tastes absolutely delicious – he's invited us all round for dinner.'

When I got the tent up, it was raining again. I resolved that once I was ensconced with the mosquito net zipped up, I wouldn't venture out until the morning. Despite getting inside as quickly as possible, there were still about two thousand of the little bastards who had managed to gatecrash. I spent a miserable half hour spraying them with insect repellent and rubbing them off my arms and hands. If it wasn't for the writing of John Irving who transported me into his strangely surreal American world of hospital abortions and cider apple harvesting, I think I would have wept with frustration. Even so, it was a long time before I stopped being bitten and then spent the night aching for a wee, but not daring to get out off the tent to let in another half a million or so.

In the morning I opened my eyes and stared at the mosquito netting inches away from my face. I could have sworn I heard thousands of tiny voices squeaking: 'He's awake! He's awake! Get ready for breakfast!' By this time I was in danger of wetting myself so I took my courage in both hands (not literally I may say) and ventured out to my alternate relief and anguish. Then I packed up as quickly as possible, bundling sleeping bag, tent and stove any old how into rucksack and panniers and pedalling away like fury. It was only when I'd got about two miles down the road that I realised I'd forgotten to pay for the campsite. You don't have to be a rocket scientist to work out that I didn't go back. If the owner of the site reads this and feels strongly that I should recompense him or her for the camping fee, I may be contacted through the publishers of this book. I will send a postal order settling my account, but I will do it with very bad grace. This time, Midge City and I are through. Understand? Through.

After cycling alongside Loch Torridon, I reached a spot where, just for once, a welcome breeze in my face blew most of the remaining midges out of my hair and clothes. I stopped, repacked my gear and pondered my next move. I had arranged to meet another old friend, Pip Hopkinson, at Applecross the next day. We hoped to do the Nose at Applecross, a classic Patey/Bonington route that must rank as the best easy climb in Scotland. It climbs a fantastically steep and exposed skyline buttress visible from miles away. I had been here once before with Gemma, who at one stage had done a fair amount of rock-climbing with me. We had enjoyed a turbulent rock-climbing relationship. Like trying to teach your daughter to drive, climbing produces the same sort of stressful situations. Most of them were my fault. On this occasion, I had just returned from an expedition to the North-East Ridge of Everest and was suffering from a persistent and revolting oriental bug that needs no further description. Whenever I ventured more than half a mile from the road I had felt so exhausted, and had to stop so often behind boulders, that we had never even reached the foot of the climb.

Meanwhile, as I had got slightly ahead of schedule again, I decided to de-midge myself properly and spend a night in a B&B in the pretty little village of Shieldaig. Then I could enjoy the ride round to Applecross in the morning. This proved to be a wonderful sunny summer's day for a change and after only a few minutes' ride I turned right onto the single-track road that followed the coast round to Applecross. The first miles were a constant switchback of steep hills and descents with hardly a yard of flat ground in between one or the other. Despite stunning coastline scenery with turquoise water, pine-clad promontories, and always the backdrop of the Torridon peaks, it was a gruelling ride round to the seaward end of the loch where the road at last flattened out and the view changed. Now the north coast of Skye was quite close across the Sound of Raasay. I had seen the island from Gairloch but the distant view was not impressive. Now I could see the Cuillin Hills in the distance and felt I was definitely making some headway south. By the time I reached the village of Applecross, I would actually be marginally south of Inverness.

Then, before too much longer, Aberdeen as well. Once south of Aberdeen, I would, I felt, be on the way home.

I was certainly riding south now. The wind was full in my face, blowing hard out of a cloudless sky. I squinted into the sun with increasing concern, for I was becoming more and more aware that I had made a really stupid balls-up. When Gemma and I had driven round the peninsula I obviously hadn't paid too much attention. Somehow I had confused Lochcarron, on the other side of the famous road over the Bealach na Ba, with its 2000 feet of ascent, with Applecross itself. The point was, of course, that I should have cycled straight from Shieldaig along the A896 and given the Applecross peninsula a miss. Now I was stuck on the wrong side and had gone about twenty miles out of my way as well.

Pip and I met at the Applecross campsite where he put up what seemed to me to be a colossal tent – we could actually both sit in it – and I gave him a brief rundown of my trip, enjoying his bellowing laughter and accounts of his goings-on back in civilisation, which meant Otley near Leeds where he lives, and Edinburgh where his girlfriend lives.

This carried us through a vast seafood platter in the pub. All that marred our enjoyment was the forecast for the morrow which was predictably foul and soon after going to bed the wind rose and the rain swept in. In the morning it was quite obvious that, yet again, we wouldn't be climbing. I asked Pip, a keen cyclist, to have a look at the Beast which in the last couple of days had started jumping gears again. He was concerned. 'You've lost three spokes from the back wheel and it's quite badly out of true.' He fiddled about with the gears for a bit, looking increasingly worried. 'I think you've got to do something about that wheel, it's not safe.' 'Something', we soon realised, meant a drive to Inverness, the nearest place with a bicycle repair shop but still about fifty miles away. I hadn't bargained for this and had to give it some thought. About ten seconds' worth actually. 'Let's do it.'

It was strange to be in a car again, particularly given the huge ascent we were making. At the top of the Bealach na Ba we were in cloud as well as the degging rain. On the descent, sandstone cliffs glinted slimily and waterfalls cascaded down the gullies. This was becoming a farce. At the foot of the pass, we rejoined the main road at a T-junction. An hour and a half later we had found a bike shop in Inverness and for the first of several occasions on the ride I was amazed at a) how helpful the service was; b) how quick; c) how cheap. It made you realise what a complete rip-off motor service garages are. The lad serving me promised the bike would be ready in only a couple of hours, which gave us time to visit an old friend from Sheffield days, Clive Rowland, who ran an outdoor shop in Inverness. We had a quick gossip and I checked to see if there were any of my books in the store (there were). Then we had a swift pint in a rather strange bar next to an undertaker's and a church. The other occupants were obviously about to attend a funeral in one capacity or another, but presumably not as the corpse, though one or two of the drinkers seemed to have been auditioning for the role for some time. Then we collected the bike which had been given a good service as well as having the wheel repaired. I had decided to fit on a pair of handlebar extensions rather like bull's horns, to give my grip a bit of variety as I rode. My right hand was increasingly numb and I hoped by changing position I might do it some good. (It made not the slightest difference.) Then we set off back towards Applecross, except I didn't get there.

When we drove through Loch Carron and into a wall of driving rain, two things were manifestly apparent. The first was that the climb was out of the question tomorrow, or indeed in the foreseeable future. The second was that there was not much to be gained by a second night at Applecross. If, on the other hand, Pip dropped me at the road junction where the Applecross road met the Shieldaig road and I cycled back to Loch Carron, he could drive over the pass and pick up the tents. I would still have cycled a few miles more than I needed, but would be spared the gruelling ride over the Bealach na Ba in the rain. Was this a cheat? I suppose so, for I had technically broken the link of riding all the way down the country. The fact that I had made a daft route-finding error should not really have stopped me, but to err is human, the flesh is weak etc., etc. I was fifty-seven years old, doing something I wanted to do for fun, and not riding over the Bealach na Ba in pissing rain when I didn't have to wasn't the worst sin I have ever committed. Anyway, if it was a sin, it was only against me. And so, with all the generosity and compassion for which I am justly famous, I forgave myself.

Leaving Pip with the unpleasant job of taking down the wet tents, I cycled back to Loch Carron, finding when I got there a hotel bar that was open. My arrival coincided with that of an elderly couple from Yorkshire on holiday. The husband seemed keen for an audience that was not his wife and regaled me with stories of his huntin', shootin' and fishin' prowess. I'm afraid I wasn't terribly interested. He had been coming to Loch Carron for many years but I couldn't help feeling that there was a fair degree of bullshit in his stories. When he started talking about the ease with which he could drive to Scotland from home and how good the motorway system was, he fixed me with a strange look. 'Course it was Hitler who built the first motorways, so he did get something right . . . as a matter of fact, I think he got quite a few things right . . .' I could see that we were never going to be bosom pals and was relieved when he included the barman in his ramblings. He turned the conversation to salmon and deer and gamebird poaching, all of which he thought was a human right – 'Just the odd one or two, nothing serious and only for your own consumption. Know what I mean?' There was a rather strained silence and the barman, bless him, quietly stated that he was a member of a local animal protection society and was an active ornithologist and conservationist. After that the conversation flagged slightly. When, to my relief, I saw Pip's car drive past, I made my excuses and left for the campsite.

That evening Pip and I returned to the bar for a meal. As the barman served us I congratulated him. 'I thought you dealt very well with your new mate, Goebbels.' The barman grinned and jerked his head. Our Yorkshire friend and his wife were sitting at the bar only feet away. Oops.

Pip, in the best tradition of the trip so far, kindly offered to take the bulk of my gear to the next campsite, for he could see no point in hanging around and was on his way home. I decided that Shiel Bridge, at the end of Loch Duich, was my next day's objective, and hoped that the campsite was obvious enough, as he would be long gone by the time I reached it. I was sorry to see Pip go. Over the years we had shared lots of light-hearted adventures in Wales, Cornwall, Lundy and of course Derbyshire. He is an active member of the Climbers' Club and a great source of gossip and knowledge. 'See you in Otley – at least it's downhill from here.'

My immediate task for the day was to ride around the shores of Loch Carron, at first with the wind, then against it. The early miles, I knew from yesterday, were flat. When I reached the head of the loch a squall blew in from the west and I sheltered behind a tree as a white wall of rain whipped up the valley. It soon faded to a gentle drizzle as I turned into the wind and started on the far side of the loch. Almost immediately I was faced with the steepest hill I had met so far. It seemed ridiculous to build a road up such an incline when all I wanted to do was follow the water's edge, but at least it wasn't too long. As I pushed the Beast uphill, a cyclist hurtled past in the opposite direction. He didn't acknowledge my presence in any way at all which I thought was a bit off, until seconds later his girlfriend (or wife or sister) also screeched past with a look of sheer terror on her face. I realised that on a wet road freewheeling down an incline as steep as this must be quite frightening, as indeed it proved on the other side.

My progress along the loch was interrupted by several of these steep hills and by my first encounter with roadworks and contra-flow traffic lights. The good news about these is that a cyclist can easily edge to the front of the queue, to the irritation of the static line of cars and lorries. The bad news is that once the lights are green the cyclist has to ride like buggery or risk being squashed by the traffic behind him, seeking revenge. On several occasions in the weeks to come I found on the longer stretches that I wimped out and got stranded amongst the orange cones as the lights changed in front and vehicles started coming the other way. The contra-flow always provided a bit of excitement, but just about all the traffic I encountered in these situations was considerate and understanding of a frantically pedalling, purple-faced old gent risking either oblivion or a heart attack. They weren't always as considerate on the open road.

At the far end of the loch I stopped in a lay-by to take a photo of the loch, now glowing in sunshine. It marked the end of what I considered to be the north-west of Scotland. From now on I would be in the Highlands. In fact, by the end of tomorrow, I hoped to be in the Great Glen and only a day away from Fort William and Glencoe. Not so fast, Curran. Even unladen, the next miles from Stromeferry across to the A87, the Road to the Isles, were a tester I could have done without. The wind blew stronger and stronger, dead ahead. The road wound up and down, seemingly leading nowhere. For the first time, I lost my temper. At every bend the road seemed to lead uphill. I ranted and shouted at the road, at lorries that overtook me, at the scenery, at the wind. Not, of course, that it made a blind bit of difference. Perhaps the worst moment of the day was going down the long steep hill to the main road to Skye. I had to pedal and when on the steepest section I tried to freewheel, I actually stopped in my tracks.

I was beginning to realise that cycling was the nearest thing I'd come across to being a baby again. No short-term memory, and an emotional range that could switch from ecstasy to misery (and back again) in seconds. At the junction with the main road at the bottom of the hill I turned left, the sun came out and a mighty wind blew from behind. The road was flat and, with a big silly grin on my face, I was effortlessly transported to that photographic Scottish cliché Eilean Donnan Castle on the end of its promontory surrounded by mountains.

Pip had told me the night before of the occasion, many years ago, when the Nottingham Climbing Club (a.k.a. the Notts Lads) spent New Year in a bothy near Eilean Donnan. Foiled by bad weather from doing any climbing, they had decided to visit the castle after a prolonged lunchtime session in a nearby bar. Finding it locked and bolted for the winter, they simply climbed the granite walls and managed to gain entry to a storeroom where, in their euphoric state, they liberated various swords, shields and pieces of armour that the lads decided must be junk. They had made little effort to conceal their crime and were duly apprehended by the constabulary. Locals were aghast that the castle, which for hundreds of years had been impregnable, had been successfully raided by a team of drunken Sassenachs. Luckily, the law was lenient in this case and the miscreants (amongst whom were several very well-known climbers) escaped with a fine of fifty pounds a head.

I had no desire to join the coach parties that were visiting the castle and sat by the side of the loch eating a bar of chocolate. It was not far to the Shiel Bridge and after the grim morning ride I was in no hurry. Ahead, I could see the glint of fresh snow high on the Five Sisters of Kintail as squalls blew over. It was hard to believe I was riding south, and into the summer, though I knew that it could and sometimes does snow almost anywhere in the Highlands right into July and August.

At the top of Loch Duich a sign left indicated a campsite two miles away up a track. It wasn't the site I was expecting and, after a moment's doubt, I pressed on to Shiel Bridge where to my joy, I found a) another campsite; b) a well-equipped shop and restaurant; and c) my panniers. The site was sodden but pretty much midge-free and I was soon ensconced in my sleeping bag, immersed in *The Ciderhouse Rules* and sipping a mug of coffee laced with the merest soupçon of whisky. I knew the next day was going to be another hard one, first a big climb up past the Five Sisters to reach the high inland Loch Cluanie, followed by another long ascent before dropping down to Invergarry and the Great Glen. But, by the evening, I would be south of Aberdeen.

The first few miles were beautiful, gaining height very gently up a flat valley with early morning sunshine lighting the contours. Soon it steepened and I could see for miles ahead as the road zigzagged out of sight. When it came to GOAP I resigned myself to a long walk. For the first time since leaving Lerwick I was conscious of traffic as more than just an occasional interruption. It was not exactly nose to tail but it was a gentle introduction to what I could expect for more or less the rest of my journey. And it would start in earnest tomorrow when I hit the road to Fort William.

Not that the thought depressed me, far from it, as I imagined that the next day's cycling would be virtually flat and I was getting fed up with the endless push up the hill. But it ended at last, and, as the first big squall of the day blew in, I sheltered behind a wall and looked at the choppy waters of Loch Cluanie. With every shower the tops of the Five Sisters disappeared and then emerged with a fresh dusting of snow like dandruff, which soon melted before the next blast arrived.

As I was still travelling due east for a few miles more I had the luxury of a following wind. But at the end of the loch I turned sharp right and started up another endless hill, this time into the wind. The view was opening up and I could see across to the still distant Nevis range. Huge snowfields on Aonoch Mor glinted in the sun but a vast black cloud behind hid the Ben itself and soon blotted out any view at all. At last I reached the high point of the day and started a wonderful freewheel, racing the wall of rain that I could see sweeping along the Great Glen. I wanted to stay in Invergarry at the junction with the A82 that runs through the Glen from Inverness to Glencoe and then all the way to Glasgow. And I wanted to get there before I got soaked to the skin.

Like the descent to the Dundonnell Hotel, this one went on and on. I passed a couple of cyclists wearily pushing low gears as they fought with gravity. There was no point telling them it was not far now, when it clearly was and anyway there wasn't time as I swept past, just like the couple at Loch Carron the day before. Then, losing speed gradually, I levelled out through pinewoods and arrived in the gloomy village of Invergarry. Before I looked for somewhere to stay, I cycled down to the road junction – my big milestone. I was south of Aberdeen and on to the main drag. I checked into a B&B just as the first drops of rain started. By the time I had carried my kit up to my room and scattered it all over the floor, the windows were shaking with each gust of wind and a continuous film of water slid down the glass. Those poor lads still battling up the hill, I thought, with a furtive little grin. Rather them than me.

9

How I Joined the Crawlers' Club

The first time I ever climbed in Scotland, four of us hired a car and drove from London to Skye. Only a few vague memories of the journey remain – waking up somewhere south of Glasgow with cows surrounding our tent and tripping on the guy ropes, stopping on the shores of Loch Linnhe and looking across to the mountains of Ardgour and, quite vividly, turning off the A82 onto the Road to the Isles. I remember it because I thought Invergarry was a sunless and depressing place then and, on the occasions I have passed through since, nothing has changed my mind. So when it stopped raining and I decided to walk down from the B&B to the hotel bar for a meal, I wondered whether my impressions were justified. I walked through the crowded room to the bar where a curt landlady instantly demanded my order.

'Um, well, I don't know yet. What's on the menu?'

'It's on the wall behind you – there's no point in coming to the bar if you don't know what you want.'

'Look, hang on, I've only just this second walked in.'

Suppressing a strong desire to walk straight out again, I ordered steak and chips. I was pointed at a minuscule table with one chair. It faced the wall and sitting there studying the wallpaper was like standing in the corner at school. Stupidly, I'd left my current paperback back at the B&B so there wasn't much to do but listen. If I turned round it would look as though I was staring (which

PHOTOCALL IN GLENCOE

would be true). The landlady was short and wore high heels. She was not light on her feet and I could judge her progress around by the incredibly loud clacking of her heels on a tiled floor, I waited, and waited and waited. Occasionally, I risked a glance and met stony-faced blankness. Eventually I summoned up the courage to ask where my meal was. The order had never reached the kitchen. I made an executive decision to move tables and sat at one where I could face the bar and had a brief battle of wills with you-know-who who seemed to be on the verge of throwing me out. As I had already paid for the meal I felt I had the upper hand, but only just.

At last a harassed and apologetic waitress appeared with my steak, which you would expect, after all this build up, would be grim. Actually, it was delicious and very good value, which doesn't seem to be the right way of ending this story. Full of food and drink I strolled back to the B&B. But I still think Invergarry is a gloomy spot.

When I left in the morning, I could hear the traffic noise before I reached the junction with the main road. As soon as I turned right I started to experience the feeling that would dominate most of the rest of the ride. It was a nasty prickly sensation in the back of my neck and it was combined with the sound of changing gears and the sneeze of air brakes. Inevitably I would scan the roadside, wondering which bit of hedge, ditch or grass verge I would be catapulted on to if the great snarling HGV behind me miscalculated fractionally. Cars normally failed to register until they had whipped past but were no less terror-provoking. Rather glumly, I realised that the peace and quiet of the past weeks was probably gone for ever.

At Spean Bridge, I met a party of End-to-Enders equipped with lightweight racing bikes, a back-up van and mobile telephones. They said they were only a day or two away from John O'Groats, which depressed me as only that morning I had been studying the map and congratulating myself on my progress.

From the Commando Memorial there is a magnificent view of

the Nevis range on a clear day. Today, being normal, all I could see was the black hump of the Ben disappearing into cloud. But on my way to Fort William I caught glimpses of the mountain unveiling itself and, just before the distillery and the track up to the north face of the mountain, I could see the whole of the north-east ridge and the Orion face.

Terry Gifford had originally set his heart on Long Climb, which is as its name implies. Now it was plastered in fresh snow. At the end of May you expect to see snowfields at the foot of the buttresses but today the mountain was virtually in full winter condition (in fact, I heard later that some of the higher gullies were still being climbed). As I had omitted to pack ice-axes, plastic boots, crampons and all the other paraphernalia of winter climbing and didn't imagine it would even cross Terry's mind to do so, I wrote the Ben off completely. I pushed on to Fort William which, given my rather spartan journey so far, was a bit like arriving in a thriving metropolis like Hong Kong, New York or Las Vegas.

I can't believe I've just written that, and if you've ever been to Fort William, I don't suppose you can either. But it really was a bit of a culture shock to be plunged into the world of shops, restaurants and bars. I found a bicycle rack and locked the Beast up, then set off to do the town. First a visit to Nevisport, which has the best-stocked book department of any climbing shop in the UK (and I don't just mean that there are invariably a few of my own in it). Then a trawl down the main street gawping like a little boy through a toy shop window at perfectly normal merchandise that I hadn't seen for weeks. I ended up treating myself to a set lunch in a dire Indian restaurant for no other reason than because it was there, as someone once said about something else. Then it was a gentle flat ride down to Glencoe. Before I left Sheffield I had arranged to meet Terry Gifford and had vaguely suggested today. Amazingly twenty minutes after I put my tent up in the Glencoe campsite, Terry turned up.

Leaving home (with an unnecessary electricity bill to follow).

The fully laden beast somewhere in Sutherland.

A bleak Shetland day, with the Drongs just visible through the gloom.

Catherine Destivelle on the top of the Old Man of Hoy with filming helicopter in attendance.

Catherine psyched up to solo the Old Man while husband Erik looks pensive.

'*Merde* – it is wet, very wet.' Catherine on the long second pitch.

Mike Banks, the oldest man to climb the Old Man, on the crucial second pitch.

Old friend and mentor Paul Nunn on Rangrik Rang.

View across the Indian Himalaya to Kamet, centre, on horizon.

The author approaching the overhang on Fionn Buttress with trepidation.

Escaping the Highlands.

Cycling under the M1 at
Tinsley Viaduct.

The surprisingly rural approach to Sheffield through the grim Rother Valley.

Gemma making light work of Covent Garden, Millstone Edge, before the irretrievable breakdown of father/daughter climbing relationship.

Damp, cramped and fed up. The author in his tent reaching the end of both his journey and his patience.

Geoff Birtles, supporter, editor and friend, nears the top of Land's End Long Climb.

Done it.

Like Pip Hopkinson, Terry radiates enthusiasm, and was soon regaling me with Sheffield gossip, plans for his next Literature Festival and various possibilities for a climb. He had also fixed me up with an interview with the journalist Steve Goodwin, about which I was harbouring vague qualms. But before that particular problem was addressed I was at first horrified, then amused, by a great horde of leather-clad bikers who arrived like an invading army on the campsite from somewhere down south. They were, in the main, on the wrong side of forty, with many an elastic band securing a greying ponytail. Almost to a man, as soon as they dismounted from their Japanese steeds, they produced mobile phones and rang home to their wives to assure them of their safe arrival. Many of them wanted to talk to their children and I bore unintentional witness to some of the sloppiest conversations I have ever heard only one side of. They seemed curiously ill at ease in a camping environment, and their conversations inevitably gravitated back to the heroic crashes, confrontations and epic journeys of long lost youth. In this respect, they were exactly like climbers, or golfers, or rugby players or bankers – in other words, any group of middle-aged males growing old reluctantly. But the thing that I found most astonishing, was that they were even in their cups quite amazingly quiet and well-behaved. Terry and I, on the other hand, made enough noise to make up for their reticence and we had a jovial evening in the Clachaig Inn.

The last time I had visited this famous hostelry was with Paul Nunn in very different circumstances in February 1995. We were supposed to be part of a team giving a talk there on a recent expedition to the Kinnaur in north India and had arranged a rendezvous at the Bridge of Orchy to grab a quick climb before going on to join some other expedition members at the Clachaig. We were aiming to do a route on what Paul referred to as 'Craig Doris' (that's what it sounded like anyway).

It had thawed all week but had refrozen in the past twenty-four hours with such a vengeance that paths, rocks, grass and heather seemed to have been French-polished. Only self-respect stopped me putting on crampons as we skidded out of the car park and crossed a farmyard, then over the main Fort William line via a railway bridge encrusted in iron-hard verglas. Cursing and slipping, we wended our way up to the crag – a short walk by Scottish standards – with Paul nursing the theory that it would be out of the wind. I couldn't see how this was possible, but Paul, canny as always, was right and, rather to my surprise, we were soon cramponing up a slope of perfect hard snow in flat calm.

Unfortunately, Paul's intended route had fallen down in the thaw since his last visit only two weeks before, and all that was left was an easy dog-leg gully. I pretended to be disappointed but dropped the pretence when Paul spotted a variation that led directly to the top of the dog-leg about three pitches from the top. It was supposedly only Grade 2 or 3, but looked ominously free of anything white.

However, the first pitch was exactly what I wished all ice pitches could be: easy-angled to begin with, steepening at the top with perfect axe placements in ice solid enough to moor the *QE2*. Above it all looked horrible: a bare gully leading to an old-fashioned cave pitch, splattered with a thin veneer of water ice. Here, for the first time in an undistinguished winter-climbing career, I observed at close hand the mysteries of torquing as Paul inserted an upside-down Friend into the cave roof, then hooked his axes into a thin crack above. After several attempts he swung up and across, front points skating on the right wall. Then to my increasing gloom, he traversed up and increasingly rightwards to find a belay of sorts. Judging from the time he took and his tone of voice, it failed to meet his exacting standards of safety.

I set off without much conviction, and ten minutes later wished I were somewhere – anywhere – else. As soon as I unclipped the Friend, the rope ran diagonally and, as I tried to pull on the axes (which felt as secure as hanging on a loose drainpipe) they threatened to pull me off. Why do I get into these situations?

'Take in – no don't. Oh Christ – watch me.' Gibbering, I pulled up, crampons skittering on what was left of the ice. Done it. I climbed up and gave Paul a bit of a look. He knew what it meant.

'Just one more pitch, Jim. It really doesn't look so bad.' Ha bloody ha, I thought as Paul unclipped from the token set of nuts and pegs that decorated the stance. But he was right again and to my relief we regained the easy gully and, after three long easy pitches, we pulled up over a half-collapsed cornice that had now refrozen solid (or so we hoped).

As usual, time had sped past and it was already three in the afternoon as we coiled the ropes under lowering skies and once more headed into the teeth of the freezing wind. A few snowflakes spat at us as we walked down a broad ridge, aiming for a snow slope that seemed to take us a long way towards the path to the farm and car park.

As we started descending the slope we caught the full force of the wind. Tread carefully, I thought, peering under my hood through whipping snow squalls at Paul in front of me. Stamping down the iron hard névé, he drew ahead. Then it happened! Suddenly I was sliding, accelerating at an almost unimaginable rate like some ghastly fairground ride. Axe in breaking position – no good, try again, but quickly before I lose it completely – a crampon catches – a crack. I spin round then come to a juddering stop in a shower of snow.

Curiously, I accepted what had happened almost instantly, with just a mild desire to run the tape back and replay the last few seconds without that nasty noise.

'Paul, I've broken something.'

'I heard it.' Paul was already plodding towards me, uncoiling the rope. 'Welcome to the club.'

What club was this?

'Well, chappie, it's not got many members and nobody wants

you to join, but you're in good company – Doug, Joe, me even . . .'

It was late on a Friday afternoon, nobody else on the hill and it was blowing hard; I twigged: I'd joined the CC – the Crawlers' Club.

'Let's just get you down this snow, then we'll sort something out.'

Being lowered down hard snow is no fun. Using an ice-axe brake to keep in control, I slid, Paul lowered. It was rather like being rubbed down with frozen sandpaper. At the end of each rope length I lay, head on the snow, axe planted at arm's length and shut my eyes as Paul climbed carefully down to repeat the process. I tried not to think too much but once, staring out at the snow-laden clouds in the gloomy twilight, it briefly crossed my mind that this time I might have blown it. I shut my eyes again.

At last, after six or seven lowers, the angle eased off and rocks and patches of grass and heather appeared. I could lose height by a combination of stomach glissades (I have an ideal launch pad for this manoeuvre) and with increasing frequency, just plain crawling. Once, I tried standing up and hopping, with an arm round Paul's shoulder but something started grating inside my boot and I gave an unmanly shriek. Paul looked embarrassed.

'Why don't you leave me up here and go down and get help? I'm sure I'll be okay just crawling slowly.'

Paul looked grim. 'Not on, chappie. It might take hours and in this wind . . .'

He was right of course and I resigned myself to a long haul. Conditions were actually perfect for self-rescue – the iced-up hillside that had been so irritating on the way up, now gave maximum assistance on the way down. Eventually we regained the path and I settled into a lumbering, ponderous crawl. It was painfully slow and occasionally just plain painful, as whatever had broken shifted about and snagged inside my boot.

(Thankfully it turned out to be only a broken fibula, not, as I had feared, a broken ankle.) Then Paul had a brilliant idea. On the smooth downhill icy path I lay on my back and crossed my legs to keep my right foot off the ground. Paul grabbed my hands and walking backwards, dragged me like a sack of potatoes. Occasionally my head banged on a rock; once Paul ripped both my gloves off.

'Sorry about that – for a moment I thought I'd torn your hands off!'

Funnily enough, the enduring memory is one of laughing. After twenty years we knew each other so well and slipped into our normal random conversations about anything and everything. Paul, knowing my capacity to elaborate, wondered how soon I would write an article about the experience. I regretted the lack of a camera.

As dusk turned to night two things bothered me. One was that I seemed to have no symptoms of shock at all and felt no different (apart, that is, from the odd spasm of pain, that produced the yelps of anguish Paul pretended not to notice). Was I already in shock? Would I suddenly flake out? It all seemed normal, apart from an almost constant desire to urinate, despite being desperately thirsty. The only other thing that worried me was the view (what there was of it), which stubbornly refused to change. Away over Rannoch Moor the faint lights of the traffic seemed miles away, which they were. My admiration for Joe Simpson in South America grew in leaps and bounds. Whatever happened, I would be in hospital fairly soon. The idea of doing this for four days, and on my own, was truly appalling.

The bumping-sliding-pushing dragged on interminably. Paul was constantly encouraging. Occasionally, he would have a rest and I'd crawl slowly ahead for a few yards. Then he'd catch up and give me the benefit of whatever odd thoughts had occurred to him in my absence. He kept telling me it wasn't too far. This was the only thing he said all day that really irritated me, as anything over ten yards was too far. But at last we came to the railway bridge. Halfway across a local train clattered past underneath, with its few occupants unaware of the minor epic being acted out just above their heads. I thought the farm and car park were only minutes away but they had obviously been moved since this morning. Suddenly, I was flagging, my knees were rubbed raw through my salopettes and now it was so flat that Paul's sack-hauling technique could be of no further help. I got colder and colder, my rests were more frequent. But at last it was done and I lay in the farmyard as Paul went to fetch the car. I looked up into the night sky. It was snowing gently and the temperature had risen.

We sat in silence in Paul's car, sipping dregs of tepid coffee from a thermos.

'Well done, Jim. Now we've got two choices – Glasgow, which is on the way home and has got big hospitals, or Fort William which is further away but nearer.'

I ignored a typically Nunnesque contradiction.

'Come on Paul, you know as well as I do what we'll do."

And so we did, arriving at the Clachaig just in time for a pint and, in my case, several medicinal drams before Paul drove me round to Fort William. Now safe and in good hands. I thanked him profusely for all he'd done to get me down. This embarrassed us both a bit. Once inside the hospital Paul, who on the hill had been in control, calm and competent, reverted to his normal clumsy self, knocking things over, stepping on various delicate bits of apparatus, bumping into nurses etc. But he had saved my life. He had also, though neither of us knew it, just completed his last Scottish winter climb. I won't forget it.

I was increasingly aware throughout my ramblings around Scotland that I was still trying to come to terms with the loss of so many friends. Not just Paul. Perhaps the solo journey was a necessary catharsis. After the death of Al Rouse on K2 in 1986, I was amazed at how many people assumed that, by writing a book about it I would have got the grief out of my system. I knew even when I left K2 with all its dreadful memories that the sorrow would never disappear. Since then, Mo Anthoine, Paul, Geoff Tier and Chris Lister had all died, a significantly high proportion of my close adult friends. I can't say that I spent every mile pedalling through a mist of tears, but in the wide vistas of the north-west, and by spending so much time on my own, I did feel to some extent that I was healing myself.

None of this put a damper on our good evening in the Clachaig, made all the more enjoyable by meeting Stephen Goodwin, his wife Lucy, and Colin Macpherson, a freelance photographer. Stephen had been writing about and around mountaineering subjects for many years and thought that inter-viewing me about my trip might go down well in *The Independent*. He had always been a keen hill-walker and an enthusiastic but moderate rock-climber. He had amazed himself (and everyone who knew him) by reaching the South Summit of Everest on a commercial expedition for which *The Independent* funded him, in exchange for reports. He had got nearly 6000 feet higher on Everest than I had managed on my one expedition in 1988 when I had only reached the Raphu La, a col at the foot of the North-East Ridge. Stephen wanted Colin to take a set of photos of the Beast and me in Glencoe the next day, which suited me fine as I wasn't feeling much like dashing off for a climb first thing in the morning.

Not that there was much chance of that. The day dawned cold and gloomy with a cloud ceiling cutting off anything remotely spectacular, which didn't bode well for photography. Feeling slightly foolish, we found a suitable spot about halfway up the pass and I posed self-consciously with the fully loaded Beast against the background of Bidean Nam Bian, Beinn Fhada and the Lost Valley. Even worse was trying to get a good climbing shot. On sodden slimy slabs, set at an embarrassingly easy angle, I tried to look the part but couldn't imagine that these pictures would ever be used. They weren't.

Much later, Stephen Goodwin and I sat outside my tent and he asked me a lot of probing questions that later appeared in the *Daily Express* as a full-page interview, complete with one of the less embarrassing shots of me and the Beast. I have to say he got to the point of what I was doing much more quickly than I have so far.

The next day Terry and I had at least to try and get a route done. He had set his heart on January Jigsaw, an easy but very spectacular climb high on the Rannoch Wall of Buachaille Etive Mor. We had both climbed the adjacent Agag's Groove, a similar but far more famous climb. Both routes are wonderfully photo-genic, perched high above Rannoch Moor with the thin ribbon of the road through Glencoe running far below. Providentially, Terry had decided that instead of a long and boring slog up a scree-filled gully to the bottom of Rannoch Wall, we would climb North Face Route, an ancient classic V Diff, and less than an hour or so from the road.

At the bottom of the climb we were joined by a party of students who had flown up from London to Edinburgh early that morning and driven to Glencoe in a hired car. How times have changed since the days of W. H. Murray, who wrote about his pre-war explorations on the Buachaille. Then, his journeys in ancient cars from Glasgow were epics in their own right. Somehow I felt that the students' casual acceptance of their jet-setting lifestyle made my own tottering progress self-conscious and dated. But before I could elaborate on these gloomy ruminations, Terry had led the first pitch and I followed him up an initial short wall.

Immediately I knew I had a real problem. My right hand was utterly and completely useless for climbing. I just couldn't hold on, not just to small finger holds but great big sinking jug handles as well. I had no feeling at all, and on anything remotely steep I quickly realised I would become a liability. I couldn't believe that I would be so handicapped and at the end of the second pitch I told Terry there was simply no point in carrying on. We abseiled off. To my chagrin and embarrassment the students obviously thought they had stumbled across an accident waiting to happen. I could imagine them using their mobile phones to alert the Mountain Rescue to the antics of a disabled geriatric. What was even worse was that I normally abseil with my right hand below the descender. Now I couldn't even trust myself to lock the rope and had to hold it with my left hand, which felt even more insecure.

Terry was so concerned with the state of my hand that he insisted on driving me back to Fort William to try and get some treatment. I remembered my arrival through the same doors of the hospital with Paul in the middle of the night five years before. At least I wasn't going to need crutches this time.

In the outpatients department I was seen almost instantly. The young doctor quickly diagnosed what Mike Richardson had suspected: a trapped ulna nerve. The only thing that would sort it out was to stop cycling. The only relief was anti-inflammatory pills that had little effect. So we drove back to the Glencoe site with a subdued Curran seriously wondering whether to give up, though I didn't dare mention this to Terry.

When Terry offered to spend the next day in support and carry my gear to a campsite somewhere near Oban, I knew I would carry on. I had already cycled over 500 miles, which was far more than I had thought possible, just to get to Glencoe, and it was far enough to make stopping a temptation I could resist. In fact it was the only one of three times on the entire trip that I seriously considered it. The first time had been on the big hill outside Lerwick, the last time would be, well, wait and see.

I cannot praise Terry and Pip Hopkinson and Geoff Birtles enough for their unstinting support. Geoff, who I spoke to on the phone at least once a week, could get quite emotional himself as he urged me on. I kept having to remind him that I was only on a bike ride; it was not exactly the Tour de France, which he watched avidly every year on TV. But it was a real help to know that my friends were rooting for me.

Terry is a member of the Outdoor Writers' Guild, which means he gets free camping at all the Camping and Caravan Club of Great Britain sites on production of his press card. So we enjoyed a free night in a luxurious campsite which, unfortunately, suffered from midges, though nowhere near as badly as Midge City. In the morning, before he left for Sheffield, we rigged a few more photos, including one of an extraordinary piece of cycle track just before a roundabout. This one was so ludicrous that it could only have been built as a joke. It is possibly the shortest in the world. A stretch of narrow track (illustrated by a crudely stylised symbol of a bike for those too thick to work out its purpose) ran parallel to the road, then shot off at a forty-five-degree angle, only to turn through a semi-circle and stop at right angles to the road again. Anyone daft enough to follow this mad diversion would end up pitched straight into the path of the traffic. We couldn't work out what on earth was going through the minds of the planners or why the road-builders hadn't had them certified for designing a road while the balance of their mind was disturbed.

Terry said his cheery goodbyes, distinguishing himself by not using a well-known phrase, and drove off carrying several more pounds of excess kit I had decided I could do without. When he left I was pensive. From here, all the way down to the English border, I would be on my own again, though I was looking forward to the diversion suggested by the couple in the Dundonnell bunkhouse and in particular the little excursion to Arran. My next friendly assignation would be when I arrived in Cumbria, probably another week away. So I'd better get on with it.

10

Battling with the Borders

I like Oban. It is a port and its waterfront has the same sort of romantic connotations as Ullapool. As I arrived, a Caledonian MacBrayne car ferry was leaving with a mournful bellow of its siren. I leant against the harbour wall and remembered arriving back here in 1988. I had been with a large team, including Chris Bonington, on a climbing holiday on St Kilda. We had chartered a converted fishing boat and suffered an appalling storm on the return voyage. I couldn't help feeling that my affection for Oban might have something to do with my heartfelt relief at being delivered onto dry land, and not, as I had feared, becoming part of the food chain of the North Atlantic.

Once Oban was behind me I would be on new ground. I would also lose a lot of the traffic, I hoped. What I hadn't bargained for was an endless supply of short steep hills, a winding road and the inevitable headwind. But the sun was shining for once and the new shapes of hills and valleys continually distracted my attention. In the late afternoon I found a good campsite overlooking the Sound of Jura. There were a few tents already pitched and I was directed to the far end of the campsite where the lady who ran it told me I had the best spot as it held the evening sun longer than anywhere else. However, I couldn't help feeling a bit of a pariah and wondered whether my scruffy appearance, tiny tent and bike represented some sort of social stigma to be kept well

MY FIRST, AND ONLY, VIEW OF ARRAN

away from the more middle-class frame tents and people carriers clustered around the washrooms and lavatories. Or perhaps, she was just trying to be kind. The sun soon disappeared behind a bank of purple cloud and it was time for paperback oblivion. Anyway, I thought, I'm as middle-class as they come.

Waking up to a new day and poring over the map again I felt a surge of optimism. By the evening, I reckoned, I would be more or less level with Glasgow and tomorrow I would arrive, and then leave, Arran. Beyond that it would be a straightforward slog through southern Scotland to Gretna Green.

The day started very much as yesterday ended, with little ups and downs of winding roads. Looking ahead it was often hard to work out where I would be travelling and sometimes I would find the road twisting into a valley at right angles from the direction I had assumed I would be taking. By lunchtime I had reached Lochgilphead and knew that the next twelve miles down Loch Fyne to Tarbert would be flat and almost straight. It was also a quite different landscape: tamer, prettier and much more affluent. The little villages and detached houses were more like Surrey than Scotland. I realised that, at last, I had left the Highlands. Reaching the pretty little port of Tarbert was like being transplanted into North Devon and I felt slightly ill at ease in its picturesque setting.

There was a camp and caravan site only a few miles further on. Before I got there I hit a landmark. I had now cycled 666 miles. I freewheeled down a hill waiting for the black magic 666 to click onto the milometer. Full of thoughts of Aleister Crowley, the self-styled Great Beast (and no mean mountaineer) of witchcraft, the Antichrist and Satanism, I kept glancing at the dial and very nearly rode straight into a stone wall. This would doubtless have raised some speculation at an inquest with such an inauspicious number providing the only clue as to the occasion of my demise.

What I had to do next morning was cycle to the Arran ferry, only about ten miles away. I wasn't totally convinced that this tiny summer service would be running, and was relieved when I turned onto the single-track road leading to Claonaig to meet a tell-tale group of about eight cars coming the other way, a sure sign that a ferry had just arrived. Needless to say, when I reached the tiny jetty it was to see it departing across the three or four miles to Lochranza near the northern tip of Arran.

I sheltered from the rain in a phone box at this rural bus stop of the ferry terminal world and, ringing Terry to thank him for his time and effort, learnt that the interview with Stephen Goodwin was in that morning's *Daily Express*. Not that there was a newsagent around, or anything else for that matter, until a little ferry emerged from the driving rain and four or five cars, plus me, rolled on. Twenty minutes later a verdant hillside loomed out of the murk and I got my first view of Arran.

We berthed at Lochranza, an unspoiled village, with a castle of the same name. Taking advantage of a momentary break in the rain, I set off immediately to ride the fourteen miles around the coast to catch the next ferry at Brodick back over to Ardrossan on the mainland. There was only one slight snag, which was that, if I had looked carefully at the map, I might have noticed that the road didn't, in fact, run round the coast but over a pass, and a monster one at that. No sooner had I started grinding uphill than the rain fell again with redoubled force. It sluiced down and within minutes it had penetrated every zip and Velcro strip on my clothing. The wind whipped puddles into a spray. My feet squelched and my socks slid in my trainers. I really, really hated that long hill. My only consolation was that there just had to be a decent downhill to get me back to the coast. I had hoped for a glimpse up to Goat Fell, the highest point of Arran; but all I saw was a sweep of grass, broken rocks and tumbling streams emerging from low clouds.

The descent was a disappointment: the road was so wet I didn't dare pick up any speed, while at the bottom a series of swinging bends alarmed me as I tried to brake gently through the surface water. Then the rain stopped as quickly as it had started and, at last, now I was on the flat, a watery sun peeped through. At the village of Corrie I stopped at a general store for a can of lemonade and found a copy of the *Daily Express* with Stephen's article in it. I had never been the subject of a full-page feature in a daily newspaper before. I had never, to my knowledge, bought a copy of the *Daily Express* either. I wondered which of my friends would see it and, perhaps more interestingly, would admit to buying the *Daily Express*. The road now hugged the coast and I passed some very baronial homes set in the lush woodland that came right down to the sea. As I approached Brodick, which is on the south side of a small bay, I could see another big squall blotting out the landscape and racing towards me. I pedalled hard for the last mile or so, trying to reach the ferry before I got soaked again.

Suddenly I had arrived in the seaside resort world of fish and chips, gift shops and chintzy cafés all seething with old people in macs. It was a bit of a culture shock. To my relief, a fair-sized car ferry arrived and I was allowed to jump the queue and cycle into the hold with its usual pot-pourri of nasty smells. The crossing took about an hour, by which time I was beginning to dry out a bit. All too soon it was time to get off and I pedalled up the ramp and out to face the delights of Ardrossan on a wet evening.

I have to say that it wasn't quite what I had hoped for, which was a quaint little port, like a small version of Oban, with pubs that did B&B, possibly a nice restaurant with a couple of tables outside, maybe even a few yachts and the odd powerboat moored in front. In fact, Ardrossan looked as though it had been left well alone since before the war (I wasn't even sure which one). The first B&B I saw had an old Ford Escort with no wheels perched on bricks in the front garden. The second, which was a pub, had half a dozen huge motorbikes parked outside. I was frightened to go in and pedalled gloomily off into a wet evening with a yellowing sky and the sodium streetlights reflected in the puddles. I followed the road to nearby Saltcoats and, as darkness fell, found a B&B on the seafront. A tragic old lady ran it, almost transparent with age, and the house appeared to be a throwback to the 1920s. My room, up in the eaves, did have a black and white TV as a concession to modernity, but only picked up a shadowy image, apparently a close-up of sugar with similarly monotonous sound effects. Not that I cared very much. All I wanted was to be dry and warm, get a good night's sleep and be out of this particular neck of the woods as soon as possible.

From Saltcoats I made the decision to go to Kilmarnock and from there down the A76 to Dumfries. It seemed marginally quicker and less of a hill road than the Galloway Tourist Route through the Glenkens. It was a bad mistake. The road was the sort every cyclist dreads, a narrow, single carriageway with a constant stream of fast-moving heavy traffic. From Kilmarnock it climbed inexorably uphill, but at a fairly gentle angle. The wind had now swung round to the south-east, exactly the direction I was travelling in. When I was riding south-west or west I couldn't complain – the prevailing wind was only to be expected. But it seemed so unfair on the few sections when I could expect help and didn't get it. I wondered if I would ever get a real tail wind bonus for more than a few miles. On this occasion, I soon felt frustrated. I had used all my cunning to outwit central Scotland, only to get onto a gobsmacker of a road where the possibility of injury or sudden death seemed ever present.

By mid-afternoon I had only reached the town of Auchinleck. A sign told me that the biographer James Boswell had been born here. Knowing Dr Johnson's lack of enthusiasm for all things Scottish, I couldn't help wondering whether Boswell's memories of his birthplace might have had a hand in influencing his views. The next town was Cumnock, which sounded like some sort of Goon Show *double entendre*. It was a dreary little place. I cycled twice round the town centre looking for a B&B but it seemed to be outside the tourist belt. The one gloomy hotel, in which I tried to book a room, was an echoing mausoleum. The proprietor curtly told me it was completely full, which, frankly, I didn't believe. I was also told there was nowhere else in the town I could stay and the nearest campsite was probably in Kilmarnock.

'Well, fuck you, Cumnock, I thought, cycling back out onto the dual carriageway. I started to look for an illicit campsite, which eventually materialised in the shape of a broken barbed-wire fence on the edge of a little wood. With a guilty thrill at outwitting the surly inhabitants of Gloomsville, I pushed the bike through a gap and half an hour later I had pitched the tent in a trampled down thicket of long grass, stinging nettles and weeds. I had a small quantity of whisky about my person and, after a rather basic evening meal, I enjoyed a wee dram as I watched a bright, northern sky glinting beyond a grim weather front of grey cloud that stretched all the way south as far as the eye could see. It was very peaceful and would have been perfect but for the distant glow of streetlights in Cumnock that reminded me where I was. Propping myself on one elbow, mug in hand, I looked through the mosquito net at the view and imagined what this would be like with female company. Suddenly, I noticed something only inches from my face. Surely not, but yes, it was a leech clinging to the net, and presumably attracted by my body heat. It wasn't as big as its Nepalese cousins, but it was enough to disperse all thoughts of any women I've ever known enjoying the romance of this spot. Actually, it didn't do a great deal for my own peace of mind, and though I flicked it into the undergrowth, there was always the thought that it might not have been the ringleader of nature's attempt to make me a blood donor. I made sure I zipped up my sleeping bag and, wishing all the inhabitants of Cumnock a nasty and painful death, I fell asleep.

I awoke to a bleak morning. It wasn't raining but the wind had got up and the weather front had moved right across the sky. When I had packed up, waded through the stinging nettles and pushed the bike over the barbed wire back onto the road I felt I had given Cumnock all the attention I could spare it in this life. Brewless and breakfastless, all I wanted was to find an old-fashioned roadside trannie, with jukebox and pinball machine, that served bacon and egg butties and lots of hot sweet tea. I wanted it to be run by a tragic beautiful woman of uncertain years who had a story to tell, yet still had a gleam in her eye – the kind of haunted woman who you wish you had met some other time, in some other place. Which was curious, because that's exactly what I did find. Unfortunately, she had a snotty-nosed child with her, and the shadowy aura of some giant Glaswegian lorry driver pervaded the café like an unspoken threat. But the bacon and egg butty and the sweet tea were real enough and, fortified by several cups, I overcame my insane desire to leap over the counter and propose to her. Instead I slunk out into the rain and cold, mounted the Beast and moodily pushed the pedals in the direction of England.

I will draw a veil over the rest of the day. Suffice to say that Carronbridge, which looked charming, wasn't, and once again I failed to get accommodation in a B&B that seemed completely deserted. As the rain continued to fall out of a leaden sky, I found another illicit campsite, this time a thin strip of land between the road and the Dumfries/Kilmarnock railway line. I have to say that by now I was very impressed with my little tent. The only water that got inside was brought in by me and I never got my sleeping bag any more than mildly damp. But as soon as I shut up shop for the night and listened to the ceaseless drumming of rain I wondered how long I could put up with this soggy existence. Without a book to bury myself in, I was sure I would have cracked long ago.

At least I had an easy ride down to Dumfries the next morning, as I followed the Nith Valley down towards the Solway Firth. The ring road around Dumfries arrived before I expected it and once I hit the main A75 to Gretna Green, I celebrated with an uncharacteristic lack of willpower and stopped at a Little Chef for breakfast. I always try to avoid these pseudo-American institutions, not just because they are overpriced and over here, but because I absolutely loathe the 'Please wait to be seated', 'Are you ready to order?' 'Is everything to your satisfaction?' intrusions on what should be a mindless half-hour of total non-communication. In any half-decent self-service restaurant, you don't have to speak at all and the whole anonymous experience can be completed in a trance. In a Little Chef, you are constantly reminded that you are in one. On this occasion, when I had paid the bill, I was even asked to fill in a questionnaire on how memorable the meal had been. I fled, fearful that if I didn't show the necessary approval I might be forced to eat another one. Before I got on the Beast, I checked the bill; a second pot of tea was described as 'Still Thirsty', which, I think, sums up the whole experience.

Leaving Dumfries, I set off on the last lap of the Scottish leg of my little adventure. After a couple of frightening miles on a dual carriageway, I turned onto a tiny B road running parallel to it. It had stopped raining at last and, though it was still cold and miserable, at least I was out of the traffic. I could see across the Solway Firth to the northern Lake District hills disappearing into soft cloud cover but I couldn't pick out High Pike, the hill behind Chris Bonington's home in Caldbeck. I was now travelling due east and knew for certain that I would arrive in Brampton tomorrow. Here, I would spend a couple of days (at least) with Jim and Marcia Fotheringham, so at the first phone box I found, I rang them to warn them of my imminent arrival. It says a lot for their friendship that they sounded absolutely delighted that an itinerant scrounger was about to descend on them, demanding food, drink and a washing machine.

It is not too hard to gather that since my departure from Arran the trip had been undistinguished, and I was sad to think I would be leaving Scotland on such a low note. So I was glad when in late afternoon I arrived in the little town of Annan and stopped in a real café for tea. The proprietor immediately suggested I wheeled my bike into his hallway where it would be safe. This little gesture touched me after my reception of the last couple of days and my spirits were raised even higher when I found the perfect B&B on the outskirts of town. I know it's a cliché to say I was welcomed like a member of the family but the landlady was so hospitable and curious about my journey that we sat in her sitting room talking for hours about anything and everything. Her husband didn't say much (he didn't get much chance) but was equally welcoming. Eventually I dragged myself away, had a hot bath and walked back into town where a Chinese restaurant promised all I could eat for seven pounds. The cuisine was average but the clientele was not what I expected on a quiet Sunday evening. A large party of locals were celebrating a birthday. Women easily outnumbered men and I became the object of some attention for various predatory ladies who were, to put it bluntly, half-pissed. They practised rudimentary advances, which mainly consisted of suggestive remarks to each other and shrieks of laughter. I have never been very good at dealing with situations like this, and tried to bury myself in my book, which I knew looked rude and anti-social but I couldn't turn on the quick-fire repartee that was called for and, in the end, I retreated shamefacedly to the B&B. At least my last full day in Scotland had been different.

With no intention of getting married, my ride to Gretna Green in the morning lacked real urgency. Halfway from Annan I was riding uphill into a strong easterly wind when a strange apparition approached, hurtling downhill towards me on the wrong side of the road. He looked like a World War 1 flying ace from Baron Von Richthofen's Flying Circus. He was dressed in black, wearing strange goggles and a pointed crash hat. He was German and quite mad. He screeched to a juddering halt in front of me: 'Ha! I haf ze wind behind me so I am riding very fast; but you haf not such good luck, Englander; for you ze war is over!' Actually he didn't say the last bit, but I wouldn't have been surprised if he had. 'I haf ridden from Newcastle and I am going to Ireland. How far is ze ferry?' I was slightly taken aback and didn't have a clue. I started unfolding my map. 'Nein! I cannot vait for zis. I must ride like zer wind while I still have it in my favour. Goodbye!' And he was gone. Very strange.

Half an hour later, I bypassed Gretna Green itself and cycled across a bridge over the M6. I stopped in the middle. A couple of hours to the south in a car would see me in Manchester and, to the north, Glasgow would take much the same time. A few hundred yards further and I stopped again at a sign that said 'Welcome to England'. About bloody time too, I thought, but it was just worth a photo.

PAUL NUNN ON THE DESCENT OF RANGRIK RANG

11

Lounging in the Lakes

As soon as I passed the magic sign I cycled joyfully down the road until I reached a secluded spot where I could get out my pocket-sized map of Britain and have a quiet, self-indulgent gloat at how far I had come. Though I was only roughly a third of the way down Britain, excluding Shetland and Orkney, I reckoned I might have done about half of the total mileage. So there was a certain spring in my toe clips as I rode the last miles to Brampton. This was combined with the excitement of meeting close friends again.

Jim Fotheringham had first crossed my path in 1993, when I spotted a tall, trilby-hatted figure wearing a pale linen jacket and trousers at the Aeroflot check-in at Heathrow Terminal 2. He looked as though he had stepped straight out of a Graham Greene novel. On that occasion he partnered Chris Bonington on a three-week trip to the Caucasus, when we all did different climbs. During various flights, walks, breaks in hotels and huts, I had enjoyed his company, and started to get to know him. Jim (when he isn't spying) is a dentist, and also a Buddhist. The following year, we were on the same expedition to the Kinnaur range of northern India. I saw a lot more of Jim on that trip as we were all climbing the same route. Then in 1997 we were both invited on Chris Bonington's first expedition to Sepu Kangri in Eastern Tibet. By this time Jim was wooing Marcia by e-mail and satellite telephone to the USA, which I thought was pretty cool.

Somehow, despite living 150 miles away in Sheffield, I had grown very close to both Jim and Marcia, who I thought was amazing. She is a gregarious dynamic lady, with loads of style and attitude. She has made the enormous cultural leap from a multi-racial high-powered urban life in New York to being the only black woman living in the Cumbrian market town of Brampton. I don't know if I could even make that jump from suburban Nether Edge in Sheffield and find it almost inconceivable that Marcia seems to cope so effortlessly.

Marcia answered the door and greeted me effusively.

'God, am I glad to get here – where's Jim?'

'He's walking Magic.'

I knew Marcia was hopelessly in love with Jim, but this scarcely answered the question. 'Yes, but where is he?'

'Jim, you're a piece of work, he's out walking the dog!'

I remembered their Alsatian puppy and before long a gigantic whirlwind of legs, tail and tongue erupted through the front door and set upon me with the intention of licking me to death. The dog was not far behind. (This is obviously untrue, Jim hasn't got a tail.)

When I had persuaded Magic that my leg was not going to be a pushover for his sexual preferences, Marcia, Jim and I settled down to a lengthy session of gossiping, aided by the first of several bottles of wine. Suddenly, I realised just how much I had missed the company of friends. I also felt the need for at least a couple of days off. Jim, as always, was keen on getting a climb in some-where, but already the big crags in the Lake District were out of the question as it had been raining for weeks. Instead, he proposed a little evening outing with Joe, his son by an earlier marriage, to a sandstone crag in the Eden Valley. This seemed like a good idea. Having been brought up on the sandstone crags of the south-east, I always have a soft spot for this rather quirky material that demands an approach all of its own. But that wouldn't happen until I'd had a bath, a good night's sleep, a lie in and an idle day in Brampton. It says a lot for our friendship that both of them were quite happy to let me do whatever I wanted and I could feel myself unwinding through the day.

The climbing trip was, for me, another fiasco. We went to Armathwaite Crag on the bank of the River Eden at the end of a rainy day. I'd never been before and was totally captivated by its setting shrouded in woodland above the gentle river. But my hand was, if anything, worse than in Glencoe and all I could do was explore the cliff for its future potential, while Jim and Joe solved a few of the classic test pieces. Joe, I was impressed to see, was rapidly matching his father, even outperforming him on occasion. It was all part of Jim's master plan to have someone to lead him up climbs in his old age. Joe was doing his A levels and had a place at Leeds University to study languages, including Russian. Presumably, after university, he would borrow Jim's trilby and linen jacket and follow in his father's footsteps.

At some point, I had to sort out my movements for the next few days in order to optimise my begging potential. I was now in the land where, if I played my cards right, I could sponge off at least three couples and ease myself through the Lake District down to Kendal where I had two very different appointments to keep. So next morning, I made some very disingenuous phone calls, reminding myself of the late great Don Whillans. He, in addition to being one of Britain's best-ever mountaineers, was a past-master at touring the country staying with friends until just before their patience ran out, when he would strategically move on to the next. My old friend Ian McNaught-Davis told me that his first wife Mary once answered the phone in their London home to hear the familiar nasal Lancastrian voice. 'Is Mac there?' No, he wasn't. 'Well, I was wondering if I could come and stay for a couple of days?' When did he want to come? 'I was rather 'oping it would be okay for tonight.' Where was he ringing from? 'If you look out the window, you'll see a phone box opposite. That's me in it."

I tried to be a bit more subtle, though there was no getting away from the fact that I was on the scrounge. But John and Rose Porter,

Chris and Wendy Bonington and Jim and Vanessa Lowther all gave great impressions that they would be delighted to see me. The only snag was that I would have to wait a couple more days in Brampton to make the timetable work out. This was fine for me as it was raining non-stop and Jim and Marcia coped bravely with my extended stay.

I realise that describing cycling uphill can be a bit repetitive, but the hill leading towards Caldbeck from the crossroads of the B5305 deserves a mention. It was absolutely straight and steadily increased in steepness. At the point where it became a GOAP the heavens opened. It was totally windless, and the rain fell in stair rods. I couldn't believe it could rain so hard; it was the sort of rain you see in Hollywood movies like *Singing in the Rain*. Bucketfuls dropped out of the sky onto my head. Any minute I was in danger of being serenaded by Gene Kelly. Soon the road became a stream and the water ran over my trainers. Occasionally a lorry would pass and its bow wave would explode over me. I can honestly say that I have never been so wet in my entire climbing and cycling life. I went through the groaning misery stage to laughing hysterically, and back again several times. There was no shelter and no alternative except to squelch on. My only consolation was to say to myself that this time next year, I wouldn't be doing this. It was a tactic used many times over the years in the Himalaya when carrying a rucksack up a long snow slope. It hadn't worked there because, more often than not, that's exactly what I would be doing a year later. But here, there was absolutely no chance that I would ever, ever, get myself involved in a long-distance bike ride again. And I still mean that.

Rose Porter was at home with her two little girls watching children's TV when a large sodden blob of Gore-tex and fibre pile paddled into her living room and stood, steaming like a racehorse, with water cascading all over her carpet. I was freezing cold and beyond all speech, except for things that children shouldn't hear.

An hour later I was transformed. Bathed, changed, dry, warm

and several cups of tea to the good. Bliss. John arrived and we quickly fell into Kendalspeak. I will explain. Many years ago John Porter, Brian Hall and I had organised three climbing film festivals in Kendal that had gone down in the annals as 'Bloody good do's'. The festival had lapsed, but John, Brian and I occasionally got together, went on expeditions or worked on films. On every occasion, normally in our cups, someone would revive the idea of another Kendal, but one of us was always sober enough to pooh-pooh it. Until that fateful evening when we all got equally pissed and woke up with a new film festival on our hands.

The first one of the revival had been in October 1999 and already plans were well developed for November 2000. I had been managing to avoid much work on this by the admittedly rather desperate gambit of cycling round Britain. Now John filled me in on all the complex sponsorship deals negotiated and the minutiae of organising the huge event that once again was threatening to become a runaway juggernaut.

By the end of the evening we were two bottles of wine to the good and as usual, had convinced ourselves that Kendal would be a serious rival to Cannes in a couple of years (though I never could picture bevies of scantily clad starlets sauntering down Kendal High Street).

I have to say I was mildly relieved not to have to go climbing with John, who is not just a powerful rock-climber, but always extremely fit. In fact, despite having been on two expeditions with him (to K2 and Sepu Kangri) and knowing him for the best part of a quarter of a century, I couldn't remember us ever actually being tied to the same rope.

But my next host, Chris Bonington, was a different matter. We had climbed together quite a lot over the years. At first in the Avon Gorge, when Chris gave lectures in the area, then in the Lakes, and a couple of memorable routes in North Wales, one being the wonderful Mousetrap on the great sea cliff of Craig Gogarth on Anglesey. More recently we had climbed in Derbyshire where, if we visited my local gritstone crags, I could sometimes show off a bit on my favourite test pieces. If, as usual, Chris had his way, we would climb on limestone, which he loves and I hate.

The most recent occasion was when Chris gave the Paul Nunn Memorial Lecture at Sheffield Hallam University and the next day was doing a major business presentation in Birmingham. But he decided there was plenty of time to visit Beeston Tor near Ashbourne and do a couple of routes. The first was just about the easiest on the crag, which I led, but Chris had his eye on a much harder climb called Pocket Symphony. It had rained the day before but the rock was dry. Chris, however, had failed to clean his rock shoes after the rather muddy easy moves at the bottom, and on the first hard section he had come flying off to his shock and my surprise. Unhurt, Chris delivered a torrent of abuse at himself: 'Bonington, you are a stupid bastard; why do I always do things that are too hard? I'm getting too old for this I'm giving up and climbing down.' Even as he spoke, he had regained his high point and, without the slightest pause in his monologue, he rushed up the hardest moves. 'This is just fantastic, brilliant climbing, what a great idea to come here – it's the best route I've done for ages.' By the time I had followed him and we had abseiled down the climb and returned to our cars, Chris was in a hurry. 'Christ, I'm going to be late – how far do you think it is to Birmingham? I wonder what time I'm supposed to be on. Gosh, that was a really good morning. Thanks a lot. Cheers, mate.' And he was gone.

Leaving John's house in bright sunshine for the mile-long ride up to Badger Hill, I knew that our original plan, which was for both of us to cycle to the famous Pillar Rock, which I had never visited, was completely out of the question. The crag needed a decent spell of fine weather to dry out, and I felt that it was unfair to waste Chris's time when I could barely touch rock anyway. In fact, it wasn't really Chris I needed but Wendy. I needn't have worried. Chris, ever forgetful, had already arranged to climb with his half-brother Gerald and was driving down to Borrowdale where, with a bit of luck, dry(ish) rock might be found on Shepherd's Crag, the nearest cliff to the road in the whole of the Lakes. I went along for the ride and the company and had an enjoyable afternoon sitting outside the café underneath the crag being entertained by the coming and going of half the Lakeland climbing scene. By the time I had chatted to all of them and drunk about ten cups of tea, Chris and Gerald had done their route. Wendy Bonington is a therapist, practising the Alexander Technique, which emphasises back posture and symmetry, as well as various relaxation exercises. She was sure that a visit to a surgery in Carlisle would help my hand and thought that the problem might originate in my neck. I was happy to try anything that might help and the next day she made me an appointment and drove me into Carlisle, retracing my *via dolorosa* of a few days previously.

After a very thorough examination of my hand, arm and shoulder, I was given some physiotherapy, culminating in a violent couple of movements which caused two almighty cracks as my head was nearly removed from its moorings. It definitely relieved a lot of stiffness in my neck and shoulders, but made no difference at all to my hand, which was now completely numb.

It was at this point that a Bonington mini-crisis occurred. Long-term Bonington watchers are familiar with these fleeting instances of human frailty in the great expedition leader's organisation and method, and equally with the way his support troops rally to man the breach. This time it was to be my turn to be called to the colours. Chris had left that morning to fulfil a commitment to Berghaus who were running a management weekend. He was due to give a presentation and, predictably, had forgotten his slides. If they could be taken to a courier outside Penrith, they would still get there in time. Wendy had an appointment at home, so I was roped in to drive over to Penrith in Wendy's car. By the time we had sorted out the insurance, time was critical. I drove as fast as I dared to Penrith. As I crossed the M6 (yet again) a driver in a show-off 4x4 Land Cruiser cut me up on the roundabout. Furious, I gave him a withering blast on the windscreen washers, and spent the next minute searching for the horn, by which time the offender had long since gone. At the company's reception desk, despite phone calls from Chris's office warning of my arrival, the name Bonington failed to impress, and it was only by luck that I happened to have the forty odd pounds in cash they demanded.

I drove back to Badger Hill in time to watch the first England game in Euro 2000, where, to my utter amazement, Wendy Bonington proved to be both a knowledgeable and vociferous TV football fan. As her husband has not the slightest interest or knowledge of any ball games, unless you count pub pool, I was amused to think of Wendy, who is a golf fanatic as well, watching *Match of the Day*.

From Badger Hill to Jim Lowther's house near Shap village is no great distance, but it provided a wonderful, varied ride. I left Wendy after a leisurely breakfast and several cups of coffee and freewheeled almost all the way down to the little village of Hesket Newmarket. Then, on a bright, sunny morning I skirted around the bottom of High Pike to Hutton Roof and Mungrisdale, cycling on a lovely little single-track road through open moorland, past one of the several Bonington bouldering spots on the way. These are clusters of rocks on a hillside, some of them quite large, that can give a strenuous evening workout without the need for anything other than a pair of rock shoes and a chalk bag. I remembered Chris once pointing out a problem that Al Rouse had solved on his first visit. Typically, it was hard fingery climbing with a potential for hurting yourself if you fell off. Chris hadn't or couldn't do it and I wondered whether he had managed it in the intervening years. The last time I had come here, it had been very wet. Chris had got stuck on some very greasy slabs higher up the hillside and I had to get a rope from the car and drop an end down to him from above. At least I think that's what happened; it could, of course, have been the other way round.

From Mungrisdale it was only a short distance to the main

Keswick/Penrith road, which I followed for a couple of miles before turning right onto a bewildering maze of lanes that led eventually to Ullswater. It is quite likely that I got lost hereabouts but it didn't really matter, I was happy to follow my nose around a beautiful miniature landscape that finally tipped me out near the waterfall of Aira Force, where I found a very chintzy gift shop which I ignored and café which I didn't.

Full of tea and buns, I pedalled easily along the shores of Ullswater to Pooley Bridge, and then turned off on to more tiny roads that led to Askham. I could see the ruin of Lowther Castle across a valley and, not for the first time, wondered at the way in which Jim Lowther, still only in his early thirties, managed the huge Lowther Estates, which stretched across the Eastern Fells. On the odd occasions I had visited Jim in his office, I had been amazed at the range of activities, farming, housing and leisure park that he was in charge of. How he combined this with a family life and still found time to go on climbing expeditions was a mystery.

With late afternoon sunlight streaming across the sheep-cropped grass of the Lowther Valley, a rural idyll, like a scene from *Far from the Madding Crowd* (minus Julie Christie, but you can't have everything), I arrived at the Lowthers' farm cottage to be greeted by Vanessa and her little girls and the dog. This trip was turning into a life of domesticity and dinners. Jim arrived shortly afterwards and soon another lovely evening of good food, drink and company was under way. I had first met Jim back in 1994 on the Rangrik Rang expedition to the Kinnaur region of northern India. From the earliest moments of the expedition, Jim had displayed the boundless energy of youth. It was Jim, as much as anyone, who had really made me feel my age. He was a very promising cameraman as well, and high on the mountain he had taken over from me on the summit day. It had been a vivid bitter-sweet experience for me, for it marked a realisation that my high-altitude career had finally hit the buffers.

Climbing with Paul Nunn, I had already surprised myself by

keeping up with the others on the lower slopes of Rangrik Rang. The serious climbing had started with a long ice slope up which we had used fixed ropes. At the top a steep traverse to some séracs provided the technical crux of the climb. I had found it exposed and very frightening but was pleased that I had got some exciting video footage of it. Paul and I reached a col to find Jim Lowther and Edinburgh climber Graham Little asleep in a small tent. For some strange reason, they had elected to climb at night, while the rest of us climbed at more normal hours. The next morning, we all toiled up to what we hoped would be a decent campsite halfway up a long snow ridge. I used my tape diary to record my impressions:

It is 2.30 a.m. I fumble with the lighter in freezing darkness. The stove splutters and its faint blue flame vaguely illuminates the cramped confines of the tiny two-man Gemini tent into which Paul and I are improbably squashed. Outside we are perched precariously on the very crest of a snow arête, which shoots away into the black fathomless depths on both sides. Chris Bonington and Jim Fotheringham share the same platform, which took three hours to excavate, though their tent actually protrudes over the north face. Just below, Graham Little and Jim Lowther have dug their tent into a made-to-measure slot, where it nestles snugly into the angle of the slope. Above us, the Indian climbers are crammed into a fourth tent. We are now at around 6000 m with only 550 m to go.

The ice melts slowly as I doze, clutching the pan with gloved hands to stop it sliding off the stove. I am hollow with apprehension. Today is our hoped-for summit attempt on Rangrik Rang, an unclimbed 6557 m peak in the Kinnaur Himalaya. Yesterday I was knackered as we climbed twelve interminable rope-lengths. Deep down I doubt I will be going much further, though I would dearly love to. Meanwhile I prepare the brew and all too soon we gulp the tepid sweet fluid and start the grim business of getting up. Paul described our interminable contortions, thrashing around inside the bulging, bending tent as being like 'two whales caught in the same net'. At last, we are ready, as the first light of a clear dawn seep through the blue Gore-tex walls.

After only one rope-length I realise that, for me, the game is up. I am going slowly and with so many rests, that I run the very real risk of jeopardising the summit bid for Paul and possibly everyone else. Sadly, I hand the little video camera to him to give to Jim Lowther and retrace my steps back to the tent, traversing precariously around it to the entrance, trying not to spike it with my crampons. I unrope and silently watch the end snake upwards as Paul ties on with Muslim [Muslim Contractor, one of the Indian climbers]. Inside the tent again after only half an hour, I lie cold and disappointed as the sounds of the others gradually fade away. It's going to be a long day for all of us.

And yet, as the sun touches the tent and the temperature rises, so do my spirits. With not a breath of wind it is utterly silent. I am surrounded with a quite fantastic array of peaks, stretching into Tibet in the north and the Garhwal and Gangotri in the south-east. Kamet is prominent in the distance, looking from here remarkably like K2. It is without doubt the finest view I've ever had at altitude and, sitting in the entrance, I lapse into daydreams and reminiscences of people and places I've been lucky enough to experience in the last eighteen years of Himalayan climbing and filming.

As I tried to digest the view, and after I had used a roll of film trying to do it justice, I faced up to some fairly self-evident home truths. Then fifty-one and on my tenth Himalayan foray, it was obvious that I could not go on making expedition films for ever. This would be my seventh. Since my first venture on the Trango Tower in 1976, I had seen and learned a lot. More to the point I had achieved nearly all my youthful ambitions, which had seemed so improbable when I first held a camera. Trango, Kongur, K2,

Everest and so many places visited, so many stories. But now sitting outside the tent, looking across the greatest mountain range in the world, I was conscious that it was time to call it a day at this level. Sooner or later the decision would have to be made, preferably by me and not the mountains.

As the day wore on, great thunder clouds, like nuclear explosions, towered over the Garhwal. Eerily, a band of haze just below the horizon crept across the vista. Since the great storm on K2 in 1986 I have been neurotic about weather changes, but could this be a harbinger of bad weather? The silence was oppressive. I melted more snow, and made a large pan of orange for the others on their return. (I drank most of it.) The shadows lengthened and the form of the ridges, stretched across to Tibet, was thrown into high relief, the colours intensified as the tent slipped out of the sun. Far below, I could see the moraines where advance base was sited. Tomorrow, with luck, we would all be back down there. But now, on my own; I could say that I was content. Tomorrow was another day.

As dusk fell and the first little pangs of worry for the safety of the others started, I heard faint voices, then, to my relief, clear conversation in the calm evening air. Soon crunching footsteps heralded the arrival of the successful team. They had all got to the top, but it had been a long day. As I passed out the orange drink to be shared by a parched Chris and Jim, my solitude was broken.

I didn't want, or need, to prove I'd made the right decision in not pushing for the summit but, descending with Paul in the morning, I almost immediately realised that I had pushed myself too hard in reaching the top camp. By the time I had descended as far as the traverse across the top of the ice slope, I was dangerously near exhaustion. In the fine weather of the last couple of days, the soft surface had sloughed off. Now all that was left was a sheet of melting water ice. The fixed rope that we had left on the traverse was no longer on the easiest line. What's more, stone fall from the rocky walls above us was beginning to rake the ice slope, one stone in fact, knocking Graham Little briefly unconscious. Halfway across the traverse, I was on the verge of falling off, I was so tired. Paul, who had been the model of patience up to then, yelled, 'You're not in fucking Nether Edge now, get a grip.' Which I suppose I did, but abseiling down the long ice slope I could barely control my legs. Near the bottom of the last abseil only about fifty feet separated me from the end of the fixed rope, tied to a ski stick on the gently angled glacier. With safety only seconds away, I suddenly realised, to my horror, there was one last obstacle. The bergschrund, the crevasse that invariably butts up against the foot of an ice wall, had been almost non-existent on our ascent and we had crossed it where avalanche debris had filled it. In the three subsequent days of perfect weather the gap had widened alarmingly and now I was faced with a ten-foot jump over a great dark abyss. I stopped just in time, right on the upper lip of the bergschrund. High above, Paul was shouting at me to get a move on. There was no way I could jump across unless I could traverse to my right for about fifty feet where the gap narrowed a bit. Paul obviously couldn't see what the problem was as I edged across. Just as I got to the point where I hoped I could jump, the snow beneath my feet collapsed, and I half-fell, half-threw myself across, landing on the far edge, on my chest and winding myself. I rolled downhill to safety and with what breath I had left shouted up to Paul, who obviously thought I'd taken leave of my senses until he shot over and almost into the gap himself. Luckily, I was still holding the rope and as he became airborne I gave an almighty heave and swung him to safety.

We spent the night at advance base and next morning descended for the last time to the comfort of base camp. Once again the landscape had changed. On the dry ice of the lower glacier, melt water had gouged out fast-flowing channels and halfway down, as I followed old footsteps, the ice beneath me broke away and suddenly I found myself being whisked downstream like an ice cold flume in a swimming pool. I knew that at some point the stream ran underground and emerged at the start of the glacier. Christ, I've got to get out of this – now, quickly. I grasped at the smooth ice walls. The problem was I couldn't stand up and was weighed down by a heavy rucksack. At last, sweeping round a bend, I hit a large boulder wedged halfway across the stream and somehow used it to stand upright and convulsively heaved myself onto dry land. In the hot sun, I slowly stripped off my sodden clothes and found that the contents of the rucksack including the video camera had remained more or less dry. Chris, Jim Lowther and Jim Fotheringham passed me, looking faintly surprised at their encounter with a high-altitude nudist. I was feeling quite shocked and descended very slowly and carefully to base camp. If I had needed anything else to persuade me to give up climbing at that level of commitment, that was it.

Now, six years later, sitting in the comfort of Jim Lowther's home and drinking his wine I had no regrets. Jim was still plotting future trips and films. He performs well in front of the camera, speaking with clarity and good sense. He could have a great future in documentary film-making were it not for his other commitments. For my own part, I had planned a modest off-road adventure to get from Jim's house to Kendal, my next port of call, and before I went to bed I examined the map closely to work out a high-level route following trails across to Kentmere. Then I slept in luxury in the Lowthers' spare room.

12

Artistic Interlude and a Warm Welcome

After enjoying the first fine day for ages, I was mildly aggrieved, but not surprised, to find that I woke yet again to mist and drizzle. I dithered about, set off into the murk, and within a couple of miles had to opt out of my little off-road project. Instead I decided to ride to the village of Shap and follow the old A6 to Kendal. Shap is a sad place. Before the M6 was built it was a watering hole on the main road north. Now it has the feeling that time has long since passed it by. As I proceeded to do the same the drizzle suddenly became a downpour and I decided it was time to put on my (nearly) waterproof overtrousers. I looked for a suitable spot and saw a driveway leading off the road. The curb had been lowered and I started turning left onto it at a shallow angle. What I hadn't realised was that a puddle concealed a bigger step than I had bargained for and as I turned in, the front wheel failed to mount the pavement and glanced off. In the split second that followed, my eye and brain registered the same sort of impressions that on-board cameras do when rally cars overturn. The horizon abruptly performed a ninety-degree twist and momentarily, the pavement seemed to be vertical. Then I registered that I had gone from perhaps 15 miles an hour, to zero in the space of a second. There was a thump of flesh on concrete and a squeal of metal on road, and I found myself lying on my side, looking at the sky.

My first reaction was of extreme embarrassment and I hoped

COOLING TOWERS AT TINSLEY VIADUCT

that nobody had witnessed my downfall. Quickly I checked out my hands, elbows, legs, and, as an afterthought, my head, thanking my daughters for insisting I wear a helmet. Cautiously I stood up. Everything on my left side hurt, but nothing seemed to be broken. The Beast appeared undamaged: the panniers had absorbed most of the shock, and probably protected me as well. Cautiously I remounted and cycled off for a few hundred yards, out of range of any shameful encounters with sympathetic onlookers, and stopped again. I had a lot of gravel embedded in my left arm and my elbow was cut, the base of my right thumb hurt and my left leg smarted, but I seemed to have got away with it. I put my overtrousers on, and still shaken, pedalled grimly off to cross Shap Fell in the blinding rain.

I suppose I must have been in mild shock for I really can't remember much about the next couple of hours, until I arrived in Kendal with an almost overwhelming desire to lie down. I booked into the first B&B I could find and, shivering violently, crashed into bed and slept. When I awoke, it was early evening and the sun was shining. Cautiously I got out of bed and was appalled to find I had bled all over the sheets. I had stiffened up and my left leg was badly bruised. I had a long shower and used all the tea bags and sachets of sugar in my room to make a strong, sweet brew and felt a bit better. Apart from missing that litter bin on the Road of Destitution, the last time I had fallen off a bike must have been nearly forty years ago and I would be quite happy if I didn't do it again for another forty (mainly because I would be ninety-eight and if by then I could still get on one in order to fall off it, well that's fine by me).

Rather to my surprise, I slept deeply again, and woke to a beautiful day and the prospect of a meeting that I had been looking forward to since I had first planned the trip. Julian Heaton Cooper is the latest in a family of artists of whom his father William was best known. His paintings have become as much a part of the Lake District as Wainwright's guidebooks, or Beatrix Potter's children's books. Julian upholds the family tradition, but his painting is about far more than the Lake District. He is a deeply serious and committed artist and one whose work I have admired since I first became aware of it over ten years ago.

Julian was a student at Goldsmith's School of Art, which has a long history of producing original and controversial artists. For years he had an ambivalent relationship with both the Lake District and the family name. There are surreal influences in his work, which is thoughtful, sometimes political and always meticulously organised and executed. The previous year I had loaned him my digital video camera when he went on a trekking and painting expedition to the Kangchenjunga region of Eastern Nepal. I had heard that he was now working on a series of new and challenging paintings. Intrigued, I went to visit him in his studio, a bleak workspace on a small industrial estate about three miles outside Kendal.

Julian welcomed me, plugged in an old electric kettle and looked around vaguely for mugs and tea bags while I stood and stared. On the end wall of his studio hung a huge painting. From a distance it had a luminous glow, almost as though it was back-lit, or was a slide projected onto a screen. It was, for want of a better description, a telephoto view of a fragment of a vast Himalayan face. Rock buttresses, seamed with snow and ice, were set against gleaming snowfields. From a distance the painting appeared super-real but as I got closer it was transformed into a mass of scumbled brush marks, scraped layers of paint and stained canvas. Retreating, the illusion gradually returned.

Now artistic know-alls will be dying to tell me that this is nothing new. All paintings do that to some extent; the Impressionists deliberately exploited rough brush marks to give their paintings their vibrancy. But Julian's new paintings are very different in that at first glance they have an almost photographic illusion of reality, and yet close to they are virtually abstract. Some of Rembrandt's self-portraits have the same effect on me. From a distance the illusion of flesh is almost tangible, but the closer you get, the harder it is to see how the trick is done. Close to the brush strokes seem obvious, even slightly clumsy. Not being an art critic all I can say is that I find this manipulation of illusion constantly fascinating.

Julian was eager to show me the whole series of Nepal paintings he was working on and for twenty minutes I was stunned and speechless with envy. I have always found that visiting any gallery I oscillate between irritability and boredom when looking at art I don't like, and feelings of dreadful jealousy at what I admire. If I wasn't so well behaved, I could have gladly punched Julian or slashed his canvas and that, for me, is praise indeed.

Conscious that Julian was aching to get on with his work, but being reluctant to leave, I kept on finding new things to look at and talk about. Julian often uses gigantic brushes, particularly when painting outside, direct from nature. The brushes are like any other artist's long-handled brushes, but look as though they are made for giants, anything up to a metre long. He buys them from a supplier in Paris and always goes over to choose them individually – one form of shopping that I could see the pleasure in.

I have always been fascinated by work in progress. Not just the painting or sculpture itself, but all the surrounding paraphernalia. Julian's studio was no exception. I was reminded of the days when I painted seriously and had always felt that the whole studio should be exhibited: once the paintings were removed and framed they obviously looked better, but the environment that they had grown out of had vanished. Later on, when I worked in film, I loved the atmosphere of the editing room, with strips of film hanging in order, dubbing charts pinned to the wall, sound tracks and cut film laced in sync on the editing bench. As with painting, the finished product, which was normally reduced to just a single aluminium can of film, didn't seem to reflect the months of work that had gone into its production. These days video editing seems to be a very soulless activity, even if the electronic techniques are basically the same. By now Julian was obviously champing at the bit to start work, so I reluctantly bade him farewell and cycled off to the Kendal campsite because I had another appointment in the town the following day.

I pitched the tent in a corner of the site next to a fence (to prop the bike against) and in a position to get the late afternoon sun. Here I idled happily, reading, sunbathing, washing and feeling pretty good. A cyclist arrived and camped next to me. He was a rangy grey-haired guy on a road bike who had ridden from Burnley that day. We got talking and I told him what I was doing. He was enthusiastically supportive and I heard him later discussing 'the bloke cycling from Shetland' with someone else. But he had shocked me by telling me that his wife had died last year. He was obviously desperately lonely and still grieving. He cycled obsessively every weekend as a way of dealing with his sorrow. It made me realise that my life could be a whole lot worse and that what I was doing was really quite self-indulgent. I went to sleep feeling suitably chastened.

Next day it was back to Kendal to do my duty by our Film Festival. I had an appointment with the Art and Exhibitions Officer, Lena Bragger, to select painters and sculptors to exhibit in November. It was a job I always half-dreaded yet quite enjoyed when we got down to it. The early festivals had shown basically amateur paintings, based very much around chocolate box views of the Lake District. Lena and I wanted to get away from this and had advertised in *The Artist* magazine in the hope of attracting a more radical approach. For the last two years we had received around fifteen to twenty applications. This year we picked six of them and were impressed with the quality of the work and pleased that it covered a wide spectrum of creative endeavour. Last year Julian had been very much the central figure, and I had been concerned that we wouldn't be having a known artist of his stature this year. I needn't have worried – the artists we chose all lived up to our expectations.

I spent the afternoon browsing around Kendal, before bracing myself for the supermarket where I was amazed and frightened by a lady who pulled straight out in front of me in the car park, drove the wrong way down a one-way system and shot out into the main road into a line of fast-moving hooting traffic. The sign on the rear window told *me* to drive carefully as there was a baby on board. I wondered how she had driven before she had given birth. Another lovely summer evening on the campsite was made even better in the knowledge that my two daughters, who both lived in Liverpool, were driving up to meet me in a pub in Kirby Lonsdale for lunch the next day. This was about twelve miles south-east of Kendal and would give me an easy hour's cycling.

I left in good time and rode out onto the dual carriageway leading to the M6. As I left Kendal I was vaguely aware of a slight knocking from the back wheel but I couldn't see anything wrong. Then suddenly there was a nasty metallic twang which combined with a flat tyre. I'd lost at least three spokes, and the back wheel was seriously out of true again. I must have done something a bit more serious than I'd thought when I'd fallen off in Shap. There was a service station about half a mile away and glumly I started pushing the Beast towards it, aware that I would now be hard pressed to meet the girls. When I arrived, hot and sweaty, I got the back wheel off and realised I couldn't possibly mend this myself. There was nothing for it but to hitch back into Kendal with the wheel and try and find somewhere on a Saturday morning that could help. I would also try and get a message to Gemma and Becky. How to do this was another matter – and Becky would discover I'd ditched her mobile phone on Orkney.

As you can imagine, my sunny disposition had all but evaporated when an angel of mercy pulled up in the form of a bloke in a car who had seen me pushing. He had driven up the dual carriageway, turned off and driven back to the Kendal turn off, turned round again and driven back up to the services to rescue me. Can you believe that, a total stranger doing a Good Samaritan act way beyond the call of duty? It turned out he was a keen cyclist himself. I was pathetically grateful. He also knew the best cycle shop in

Kendal, which luckily was on the way in, and he let me use his mobile phone to leave a very optimistic message with the girls' Mum (i.e. my first ex-wife) who thought they might just phone. I can't remember feeling so impressed with man's greater goodness. I hope he reads this. The bloke in the bike shop was apologetic and said it might take up to an hour to fix. Only an hour and he was apologetic! He also charged the colossal sum of eleven pounds for his labours.

By half past eleven I was walking out of Kendal holding the repaired wheel in one hand and hitching with the other. It seemed to me to be pretty obvious to the passing traffic that I was only looking for a short lift to a stranded bike, but I was quite surprised at how long it took before someone stopped, which merely underlined how lucky I had been earlier. But in the end a car did pick me up and I was dropped off ten minutes later at the services. I now had only about half an hour to get to Kirkby Lonsdale. About a mile down the dual carriageway, I rode past a car that had broken down. It wasn't on the hard shoulder and was in real danger of being rammed by passing traffic. Its occupant was a mildly hysterical lady, desperately trying to contact a garage on her mobile phone. Having had the benefit of help so recently myself, I couldn't pass by on the other side (well the same side actually) and I stopped and helped push the car to a safer place, horribly aware that at any second I could receive a ten-ton lorry up my arse.

In a sweaty flurry I eventually found the right pub in Kirkby Lonsdale where Gemma and Becky had got my message, so were reasonably relaxed about my late arrival. I was incredibly pleased to see them and felt quite emotional. They wanted to know my news, but not as much as I wanted to know theirs, particularly Becky's, who was engaged to be married at the end of the year. Usually I would have found these pre-marital arrangements of only peripheral interest, but I was clearly in need of a quick fix of domestic normality. Full of paternal bonhomie and two pints of lager, I cycled drowsily through the heat of the afternoon to Ingleton and checked into a pub that did B&B.

When I woke up to another hot day, I realised three things. One was that I really wasn't too far from home; second, that my hay fever could start any day now; and third, that I hadn't thought through either my route or time scale back to Sheffield. Ever since I had set out, Geoff Birtles had told me he wanted to cycle out to meet me and give me an escort into Sheffield, and I had always imagined that I would ride in through North Derbyshire. But, looking at the map, I wasn't so sure. All the major roads in the Manchester/Leeds/Sheffield triangle run east to west, not north to south, and any route from North Yorkshire would be complicated and very hilly. Pip Hopkinson, who lives in Otley, suggested I simply rode right around north of Leeds and then down the flat roads east of the A1 and enter Sheffield via Doncaster and Rotherham. I was slightly reluctant to do this as I had fantasised about freewheeling down Ringinglow Road from Stanage Edge to home, rather than cycling through the grim Rother Valley; exactly the route I had travelled by train on my way up to Scotland, a journey that now seemed to have happened in another lifetime.

Today, riding away from Ingleton towards Skipton and Otley, it was make-my-mind-up time. Another complication, which I couldn't really understand, was that Geoff was insistent that I arrived on a Saturday morning, which gave me six whole days to get there. At that moment, with the temperature soaring, this wasn't a problem and I decided to spend a day in Gargrave enjoying the sunshine. Gargrave is a pretty little village in the Yorkshire Dales. The Pennine Way goes through it. It has a café frequented by cyclists. It also has several good pubs. My mind was made up. The eastern route it was.

It probably seems odd to read that I was complaining of fine weather, when for the last two or three weeks I had done nothing except moan about the rain. The real problem was not so much the heat, but my annual attack of hay fever. Those who don't suffer see it as a bit of a joke affliction; those who do, need no enlightening. I knew that for me the crucial time is from mid-June to early July and I had no intention of cycling through the English countryside in a welter of tears and snot. Now I was only days from some sort of sanctuary at home in Sheffield and the first symptoms were just beginning to make themselves felt. Ironically, a good shower of rain would clear the air and give me, literally, some breathing space. By the time I reached Gargrave, I was hot, dusty and sneezing constantly.

The next day was the hottest day of the whole trip. Not a breath of wind and a cloudless sky. I had no desire to go anywhere and lay in the sun reading, or in the tent trying to get a bit of shade. My only movement was to buy some anti-histamine pills in the village and to ring Pip in Otley. In doing so I left my Filofax in the phone box, never to be seen again and cutting me off from dozens of friends and business contacts that a year later are only slowly being renewed. This means that if you think I should have contacted you in the last year and haven't, you now know the reason why. Later I endured a stiflingly hot night. Even with the tent wide open and my sleeping bag unzipped and used as a duvet I was hot until about five in the morning when I awoke to the familiar sound of rain pattering on the fabric. Hastily I zipped up the door and in the grey dawn light watched the raindrops running together and trickling down the side of the tent. At least I'd stopped sneezing

The rain didn't last long, but it did clear the air and by mid-afternoon I arrived in Otley and was banging on Pip's back door. I was back in begging mode and realised that with luck I wouldn't have to camp again until the last chunk of the journey, from Sheffield down to Cornwall. Pip had made an impressive curry, which wasn't just good but didn't involve me in any way at all in its production, which was even better, as I was immersed in the first episode of *EastEnders* I'd seen for weeks and was trying to work out what was going on.

Pip had decided that he would cycle with me on the next short stage of my journey, to his brother Nick's house in the tiny village of Tockwith between Wetherby and York. There was no hurry either to get up or leave in the morning, and plenty of time to read the papers and drink coffee. It was so civilised I really didn't want to go anywhere and procrastinated for as long as possible. Apart from anything else, Pip had a road bike, was riding unladen and was probably fitter than I was, and I didn't relish any sort of competition which, even for old farts like us, was almost inevitable. In the end, we managed to get going and, after leaving Otley, my spirits rose. Pip had worked out a great alternative route to his brother's, riding almost exclusively on minor roads all the way. With the west wind behind us, it was a joy to be cruising through the Yorkshire countryside, until we met a section of short sharp hills in which my worst fears were realised as I got several views of Pip's bulging calf muscles receding into the distance as I dismounted and pushed. But he was very considerate and always waited for me at the top.

When we arrived at Nick and Jill's house, I was in the company of two keen cyclists. Once again I was having trouble with the tension of the gear cable. Nick, being a dentist and presumably mechanically competent, and Pip, with a background in engineering, were both eager to do a spot of tinkering. I was sure that their combined talents could sort the problem out. They didn't, and I spent a frustrating half hour as the light faded riding round in circles outside Nick's house like Paul Newman but without the tricks, while the chain jumped from one cog to another. In the end they managed to get it back to no worse than it had been before and we retired inside to enjoy what was left of the evening in a more civilised and better lubricated manner.

Before I went to bed Nick told me about a cycleway that had been opened from York to Selby along a disused railway line. It was part of a nationwide network of routes that one day might enable a cyclist to ride virtually all over the country without using the roads. It sounded like a good idea and I tried to understand Nick's directions to the beginning of it. Needless to say the next morning, cycling round the outskirts of York, I got lost. Cycling in the rain along a busy dual carriageway, I was following a marked cycle lane which was only about eighteen inches wide and provided with raised drain covers every fifty yards or so. Hitting one of these, the handlebar bag containing camera, maps, wallet and valuables bounced off, luckily falling clear of the wheels. I stopped and retrieved the contents to an accompanying barrage of blaring horns from passing lorries, who kindly refrained from shunting me into oblivion. Cursing dual carriageways, lorries, rain and everything else I could think of, I remounted and pressed on in a really vile temper until my rage was almost immediately alleviated when I passed the 1000 mile mark on my milometer. I guessed that the total journey would now be around 1500 miles.

Soon after that morale-boosting milestone I found the right road onto the cycle track and rode peacefully through the farmland to Selby. As it was along a disused railway line it was both flat and straight. It was also infinitely safer than the dual carriageway but I have to say it was mildly boring as I didn't see a single soul for the entire twenty-odd miles. It petered out on an estate in Selby and all too soon I had rejoined the traffic as I started on the last but one section to Sheffield and home.

I was still too early for Geoff's specific rendezvous on Saturday morning, so I decided to drop in and visit Laraine, my second ex-wife, and Mike, my old climbing partner and cycling adviser. They lived in the little village of Barnburgh, near Doncaster, and from there it would be an easy ride back into Sheffield. Laraine had a girlfriend who memorably told me that I would have lots of good antidotes to tell them when I'd finished my journey. I wondered if there was something in the air in this particular part of South Yorkshire that provoked curious figures of speech, for in the past, Laraine's mother had observed her cat 'pruning itself', and Laraine had once told me with depressing accuracy that 'I wanted my jam buttered on both sides.'

Geoff Birtles had arranged to meet me at midday in the curiously named Foljambe, a large pub in Rawmarsh, east of Rotherham, with a friend of ours, Ian Campbell. From there we would ride into Sheffield on another cycleway along a system of canals.

I was beginning to take for granted that our rendezvous would be on time, as all the others on the trip had been so far, so I was not really surprised when we all arrived simultaneously in the huge pub. The landlord kindly allowed us to bring our bikes inside: I doubt whether they would have lasted ten minutes outside and I was still tempted to lock mine up. After a couple of pints we joined the towpath leading towards Sheffield. It was situated right next to a former British Steelworks, now called Corus, which I couldn't help thinking of as 'Car rust'. I was sure this ride would be a farce, but it turned out to be one of the most amazing sections of the whole journey. Once off the road, we could have been in the depths of the countryside as we pedalled sedately through what looked like an almost tropical landscape with only distant glimpses of the industrial devastation I had noticed from the train on the way up to York. Along each side of the towpath old men sat fishing for supermarket trolleys and old prams. (Not really. I saw plenty of landed fish that had presumably been caught, not brought from the local Tesco.) Perhaps the most incongruous section took us under the M1 viaduct at Tinsley. Lorries thundered overhead as we pedalled happily along the verdant canal banks, overhung with fig trees. (This is true.)

A particularly welcome sight for me were the two huge cooling towers flanking the motorway, a well-known Sheffield landmark. I have always liked cooling towers, a twentieth-century masterpiece of design simplicity. I can never understand why they are so often used as a symbol of pollution and presume that the media simply don't realise that the clouds of steam rising from them actually form drops of distilled water, about the purest industrial by-product imaginable.

Approaching Sheffield from the east, as M1-users do, is probably why it still retains a reputation for being a dirty old steel city. But its western suburbs abut the edge of the first National Park, and there are literally thousands of rock-climbs and hundreds of miles of footpaths and bridleways within twenty miles of the city centre. No wonder Sheffield has more climbers living there per square mile than any other city in Britain (or possibly anywhere else). I was amused to read that the mountain writer, novelist and essayist C. E. Montague, should have written the following in 1922: 'Who so base as live in Sheffield? . . . With all the delectable mountains of the world to feed on, what but some defect of nature or some taint of blood can make men wilfully elect, like the elder Hamlet's misguided widow, to "batten on this moor"?' Perhaps he didn't enjoy hand-jamming.

As we reached Sheffield city centre, Geoff speeded up. I knew we were going to celebrate with a pint in the Sheaf Quay and couldn't quite understand why he was dashing off to get his round in. Then the waterfront came into view and I freewheeled the last few yards to the pub entrance, dismounted and, just as I was about to go inside, the door opened and a flood of friends burst out to welcome me. I was quite overwhelmed and I realised why Geoff had been so insistent that I arrived on a Saturday. I couldn't believe that nearly everyone I cared for in Sheffield should have made the effort to come down to the city centre.

There was, of course, just one slight snag which I felt I had better mention: 'It's really kind of you to do this, but I haven't finished yet. There's still another 400 miles to go.' My protests made no difference and I had to refuse numerous offers of drinks if I were to ride the last couple of miles home without being done for being drunk in charge of a bicycle. Eventually I tore myself away and pedalled slowly up to Nether Edge. I opened the front door to a small avalanche of junk mail and bills amongst which was a postcard from my old friend Mac that simply said, 'You persistent old bugger.'

13

Pedalling the Peak and Wandering Wye

Once I had arrived home my hay fever blossomed, even though the wettest summer weather since seventeen something was well under way. On the Monday morning I took the Beast back to W. E. James Cycles. They had promised to give every new bike sold a completely free service after one hundred miles, but they generously turned a blind eye to the fact that I had now done over a thousand. To my delight, they had a large backlog of work and said it would take a week, which suited me fine. I felt I needed a complete service as well. I could sleep for England and kept well clear of the gym or any form of exercise, except for one evening when Terry and I went out to Stanage Edge to prove, as if I needed to, that my hand was still quite useless for climbing.

One Saturday evening I had a barbecue in my back yard. Lots of friends came and before they arrived Geoff Birtles gave me a poster of the British Isles on which I traced my route so far with a red marker pen. It would stop having to tell people over and over again where I'd been. The next day, when the debris was cleared and my hangover allowed it, I cast a jaundiced eye over the map and forced myself to address a few questions.

If I was really honest, the best part of the journey had been in Scotland, though individual days since had been enjoyable. But there was now not much ground I hadn't already covered before and, with no real possibility of any more climbing, there

BLACK SLAB, STANAGE; SCENE OF A FAMILY FALLOUT.

certainly wasn't a great deal of point in cycling across to North Wales, as I had originally intended. I was tempted to get on the bike and just go as fast as possible to Cornwall. Somehow, this didn't seem very satisfactory either and for a few days I tried to work out exactly what I did want to do for the rest of the trip. I didn't want to complete the journey just because I had to. I didn't want to give up either, but with each day that passed I could feel my willpower ebbing away. It rained every day and though I was ready to leave again it was all too easy to put it off to some indeterminate date in the future. The euphoria of getting home was slowly turning into guilt at being there. At least my hay fever was subsiding and I would soon be free for another eleven months.

In the end I decided to make a move and slowly repacked the panniers on my bike that, since its service, seemed like driving a Rolls-Royce. Two nights before I left I walked down to the Brincliffe Oaks, my local pub, for a couple of pints and a chat to the team that invariably assembled on Thursday evenings. Rab Carrington, who manufactures the justly celebrated 'Rab' down clothing and sleeping bags, looked at me sternly through his piratical beard and thick glasses. After a few seconds' thought he proclaimed in his Glaswegian accent that at least it was downhill all the way from here to Cornwall. I was lost for words.

The next night I slept so badly that I gave up trying and got up before six to have breakfast and check that I had left the house in order. Leaving this time was even worse than the first, though I knew that all I was going to do initially was cycle across the Peak District to visit Becky and her fiancé, Bob, who had moved from Liverpool and bought a house in Altrincham. My plan was to cycle down through Cheshire, Shropshire and Hereford and Worcester to the Wye Valley and reach Bristol via the Severn Bridge.

It was a grey muggy morning but not actually raining when I locked up the house for the second time. I amused myself within fifty yards of setting off by riding along my own little section of suburban insanity. This was a piece of cycle track in Nether Edge that had been constructed (after several false starts) at the same time as a traffic-calming scheme had been introduced. The latter took the form of speed bumps which, even as a motorist, I felt were both necessary and welcome. However, the cycle track from the corner of Edgebrook Road to Union Road was an even worse example of council profligacy than the one near Oban. This particular aberration, which went round a gentle bend from one quiet road to another, was all of eighteen yards long and, as far as I could see, served no purpose whatsoever. I have never, in the five or six years since it was built, seen a single cyclist using it. Maybe I was the first.

Once I had mastered this hurdle I rode out of Sheffield the same way that I had taken on my first mountain bike venture to the Moon, years before. I have to say that whatever fitness I had gained in the previous thousand miles seemed to have completely evaporated after my break. I ground my way up to the top of the hill leading down to the Foxhouse pub. Just before I started the freewheel, a group of cyclists swept past on the other side of the road. One of them stopped and turned round. In his cycling helmet and trendy sunglasses it took me a minute or two to recognise Clive, an instructor from the Body and Soul Gym at the YMCA. I was delighted to see him, not least because he had seen evidence that I was actually doing what I had told him when I persuaded the gym to defer my membership until I returned. He wished me luck and sped back towards Sheffield as I plodded onwards towards Hathersage.

It was a trip down memory lane for me, for I was cycling through the Eastern Edges. To the south were Froggatt and Curbar, to the north Burbage and Stanage and immediately in front of me Laurencefield and Millstone Edge on either side of Surprise View where the road swings to Hathersage. I have been climbing here for the best part of thirty years and most of my deepest friendships were forged on the rough gritstone crags and slabs of Derbyshire and Staffordshire. I couldn't help smiling as I glanced up at the square-cut corners and arêtes of Millstone Edge. I had been sorting some slides before I left and found a series of stunning shots of Gemma, my eldest daughter, climbing an exposed wall. As I have already mentioned, the father/daughter relationship certainly didn't help her climbing and it reached its nadir one weekend on Stanage in front of a crowd of 'celebs' gathered worldwide for the British Mountaineering Council Conference in Buxton. I had led Gemma up the old classic, Black Slab. She had climbed the crux, which is quite low down, with no trouble at all, and was on the easy upper section when she unaccountably froze.

'Come on, Gem,' I cajoled. 'It's dead easy, just step up with your left foot.'

'Fuck off,' was the cryptic reply.

'Gemma,' I hissed, aware of the audience, 'remember who you're talking to.'

'Fuck off, Dad,' she corrected herself, to the delight of the spectators. Later on an American climbing magazine reported our exchange with great glee as yet another example of the eccentric ways of their curious climbing cousins.

I rode through Hathersage, Hope and Castleton, resisting the temptation to stop at numerous cafés and cycled towards Mam Tor, the Shivering Mountain. The road now takes the narrow defile of the Winnats Pass but used to skirt the base of Mam Tor in a set of sweeping bends like some miniature Alpine ascent. When I had first driven across Derbyshire it had been the normal route for me to visit my in-laws from my first marriage. The road, rather like the marriage, was in a constant state of repair, and both gave up the ghost at about the same time. These days it is possible to walk or mountain bike up the remains of the old road, which looks like something from the San Fransisco earthquake. Faded white lines are still visible with great steps or drops in the broken surface. It is hard to imagine these sorts of forces at work in Britain, the explanation being that the road was built on a major fault line. To the north is the Dark Peak, of gritstone edges, peat bogs and heather moorlands. To the south is the White Peak, a plateau of limestone tors, drystone walls and deep-cut dales. The old road ran exactly up the middle of this and, in the end, nature won. But it was an exciting little ride/push/scramble and I emerged to rejoin the road from the top of the Winnats well exercised.

The A645 runs along below Rushup Edge above which hang-gliders and parapentes do their stuff. When the road starts descending towards Chapel-en-le-Frith it passes something called the Chestnut Centre. For years I imagined a group of unsuccessful comedians sitting around telling each other weak jokes to put in Christmas crackers. In fact it is a sanctuary for otters, rare owls and injured animals. I had visited it once a few years ago with Hugo, the son of an ex-girlfriend, and I remembered that I would be seeing him briefly in a couple of days' time. I had known him since he was under a year old – now he was eleven. Though I only see him very occasionally, I try and keep in contact, not least because he is an extraordinarily talented musician, and every time we meet his skills have progressed in leaps and bounds.

My map wasn't detailed enough to guide me across the southern suburbs of Manchester, so I navigated a maze of small roads through various estates by looking at the planes landing at Manchester airport and found what I imagine must be the shortest possible way to Bob and Becky's new house and a great family evening which Gemma had driven over to join. The weather had steadily improved as I rode over the Peak, and next morning was a perfect summer's day as I cycled gently out of Altrincham, aiming for Knutsford and the Cheshire Plain. I rode down minor roads, under the M56, and soon found myself pedalling through the little village of Mobberley. Every few minutes jets taking off from Manchester airport roared overhead, bound for all corners of the globe. A strange juxtaposition, I thought, as I passed the old parish church. For it was here, over one hundred years ago, that the young George Mallory first started his climbing career on the church roof. Air travel was unknown and when Mallory left for the first Everest Reconnaissance expedition in 1921 it took five weeks to sail from Tilbury to Calcutta. Today, a 747 lumbering into the air above the square stone tower of St Wilfred's parish church would be touching down in Delhi only seven hours later.

Going through Mobberley reminded me of the still unresolved Mallory and Irvine enigma. When the frozen body of Mallory was found on Everest in the summer of 1999, I had heard the news while driving up the M1 on a quiet Sunday morning and had been shocked at how emotional I had felt. Since I was a small boy I had been fascinated, almost obsessed, with the fate of Mallory and Irvine, lost on Everest in 1924 and last seen by Noel Odell high on the North-East Ridge of the mountain before being hidden by clouds. Years later I had written an optimistic treatment for a drama-documentary about the two men that hadn't got anywhere. But after the discovery of Mallory and subsequent controversy about the publication of photos of the body, eerily preserved like a Greek statue, a number of books on the subject were published which I found myself reviewing for *High*.

All the books dealt reasonably accurately with the facts up until the discovery of Mallory's body. He was found face down with arms outstretched, at a height of over 27,000 feet, more or less in the fall line of an ice axe found about 900 feet higher in 1933. The axe almost certainly belonged to Andrew Irvine, and its discovery had led to the speculation that it marked the site of an accident. Frank Smythe, a member of the 1933 expedition, thought even then that further traces might be found on the terrace of snow and scree, which was exactly where the body was discovered. But finding Mallory did not provide any more evidence of what had happened.

It is likely, maybe probable, that the accident occurred on the descent – Mallory's oxygen set was missing, which, unless it was torn off in the fall, he would almost certainly have been carrying on the ascent. His snow goggles were in his pocket, suggesting dusk or nightfall, but even this is not certain. He must have been still roped to Andrew Irvine, judging from the coils around his shoulder. A broken end suggests a catastrophic fall, causing it either to break under the strain or be cut on projecting rocks. But who fell first and why is still not known. Andrew Irvine's body may or may not be similarly preserved nearby, which may give further clues by the time this book is published. Another expedition is being mounted in the spring of 2001 to search for him. There is a tantalising possibility that a camera on the body might just yield photos of the couple's last climb, including the very remote chance of summit shots.

What I and many others had found irritating and distasteful was the immediate publication of the photographs of the body in the tabloid press. 'The Photos That Show That Mallory Climbed Everest' was one outrageous headline. But even those who should know better came out with theories and speculation that were equally ignorant, hopelessly optimistic or just plain mad. What was worse was that some of the books, having propounded their theories, managed by some not very subtle sleight-of-hand to turn them into facts. In particular, believing Mallory could have climbed the famous Second Step, when Odell may (or may not) have caught his famous last sighting of them, seems to have become almost a matter of religious faith. Like the Dead Sea Scrolls, experts pored over every syllable of Odell's writing, searching for hidden meanings that were never intended. I personally fervently hope that the mystery is never solved and that Andrew Irvine's body remains undisturbed and undiscovered.

Contemplating this whole fascinating saga, the miles unravelled fairly easily and Knutsford, Holmes Chapel, Sandbach and Crewe slipped past almost unnoticed. In the late afternoon I arrived in

Nantwich and found a surprising little campsite, almost in the middle of the town, in a corner of a public park. It was a painless introduction to the first night under canvas for weeks and I quickly relapsed into the familiar ritual of brew, meal, another brew, paperback and sleep. The first couple of days out of Sheffield had gone well and I felt I was back in my travelling element once more.

Could it be that the weather was picking up at last? In the morning I walked to the toilet and washrooms through heavy dew. The flysheet was quite sodden. It was the sort of day in which you are just happy to be alive, and later I pedalled easily south, through the rich Cheshire and Shropshire farmlands, feeling at one with my surroundings. While I had been at home I had read a pretentious and deeply stupid article in a Sunday paper claiming that the British countryside was an illusion and just a distant memory of a totally urban society. I wondered if the writer had ever left London in his life. As I rode I could see the outlying Welsh hills on my right, and ahead was the distant view of the Stiperstones and the Long Mynd. I was pretty sure it wasn't an illusion.

I had hoped to camp somewhere around Church Stretton after meeting Hugo at his grandparents' home, but as I rode into Shrewsbury I realised that yet again I had broken a couple of spokes on the back wheel. I was now quite conscious of the need to look after the Beast and knew that a town the size of Shrewsbury would have a decent bike shop somewhere. There might not be another one before Bristol and I couldn't take the chance of pressing on without getting it fixed.

I rode slowly up an unmade road on Bayston Hill with superb views over mid-Shropshire to the house where Hugo's grandparents lived and spent a magic hour or so with him as he played his saxophone with dazzling skill, then transferred to the clarinet which he had only just taken up, and ended with a little piano recital. My daughters are talented musicians, Becky in fact, did a degree in music at Edinburgh University, but Hugo is in a different league. I can't help wondering where his talents will take him and hoping he finds a fulfilling career. As my father was a musician (he was a violinist at the Royal Opera House, Covent Garden), I know how difficult it is to earn a living out of music alone.

Before I left, I showed Hugo the Beast, which he described as 'cool' and, wondering when our paths would next cross, I cycled off, to find a corner of a nearby field to camp illegally in. It was a beautiful calm evening and, as I sat in the still warm grass outside the tent, a couple of dogs bounded up and greeted me ecstatically. Their owner, a county lady in a Barbour waistcoat and sensible shoes, strode past pretending I didn't exist, and I half expected to be moved on by an irate farmer or even by a policeman, but my fears were unfounded.

In the morning I cycled back into Shrewsbury as soon as I thought the shops would be open and found yet another brilliant and helpful bike shop. I was told, once again, that they would only take an hour or so to sort out the back wheel, which was quite badly out of true. There was a pleasant café opposite and I drank coffee, ate croissants and read *The Times* until it was time to collect the Beast. The bike shop owner said he thought I ought to get the wheel completely rebuilt, or even buy a new one, but it should see me down to Cornwall. I had told him what I was doing and, to my amazement, he asked me if I was halfway there yet. This was despite having a large map of Britain pinned to the wall behind him. I pointed out where Shrewsbury was in relation to Scotland and he seemed quite surprised that there was so much country to the north. As far as I was concerned, Shrewsbury marked almost the end of the Midlands and I hoped by the end of the day to be in Leominster. Tomorrow I would be in the Wye Valley and the day after should see me in Bristol. Was I halfway? Was I, buggery – I'd nearly finished.

By the time I got going again it was mid-morning and the sun was blazing out of a steely sky. I rode towards Church Stretton, momentarily regretting a turn-off that led to a lost love and, a few miles later, another one that led to the home of two elderly cousins, both of whom were now dead, who had been very dear to me when I was young. I found it strange that none of the three could possibly have known that my thoughts were with them as I passed, and only one could ever find out. However much I still cared it was wasted emotion. As with my lost love in Sheffield, there was absolutely nothing I could do to change the situation but the hurt was still there. Cousins Chris and Sheila and Hugo's mother were never ever going to be part of my life again.

Church Stretton, Craven Arms, and Ludlow all set in the heart of the English countryside, passed almost in a dream. I'm sure I'd driven this way before but felt I was seeing everything for the first time. The day turned into a golden P. G. Wodehouse sort of afternoon and I felt I could carry on for ever. Instead I stopped in Leominster, found the Tourist Information Office, and asked where the nearest campsite was. The answer was that there wasn't or didn't appear to be one and there was much scratching of heads until the lady I was talking to remembered that on the way out on the Hereford road was a house that did B&B. The owners allowed camping in the back garden, which sounded curious enough to go and have a look.

Sure enough, there was a small sign to that effect in the driveway of a very ordinary suburban detached house. There was a car in the drive, but no answer when I knocked on the front door. The next-door neighbours said they would probably be back in half an hour, so I settled down to wait, and wait. I decided I might as well put the tent up while I waited, then rode back into the centre of town for fish and chips. When I returned there was still nobody at home and I have to say I felt more than a bit foolish lying in my tent on the lawn in the back garden, next to the flowerbeds. It got dark and it was obvious the owners weren't coming back. I slept well but woke early with the nagging feeling that I was trespassing. There was still nobody in and, peering through the letter-box, I could see a pile of unopened mail; I packed up and left, unsure whether or not to shove a fiver through the front door. In the end I didn't. After all, I had only rented a patch of grass, as there was no water or facilities available. But if the owners make contact, I'll pay up.

About two miles down the road, I had what I had come to call a CRAFT moment (Can't Remember a Fucking Thing). Where was my wallet? I stopped on some waste ground and looked through my handlebar bag to no avail. I was convinced I had left it at the chippy, or that it had fallen out of my pocket onto the road. With a horrible sinking feeling I decided to ride back, but first, as a final gesture, tipped the panniers out onto the ground. The wallet was right at the bottom. What on earth possessed me to bury it underneath everything when I needed it every day? It was, I suppose, more evidence of impending senility, but as usual when I find something I thought I'd never see again, I felt as though it was my birthday, and rode off in great good humour.

My joy lasted all the way to Hereford, which I'd never been to before, and the shade of the cathedral beckoned. In its cool interior I looked at the frayed and faded banners of the local regiments and wondered, not for the first time, how the church could reconcile Christ's pacifist exhortations to turn the other cheek, forgive your enemies and love thy neighbour with the slaughter and barbarism of war, and an obvious pride in armed forces. Don't get me wrong. I'm no pacifist and believe, for instance, that victory in the Second World War was possibly the biggest blow for the cause of freedom that the world has ever seen. But I'm not at all sure that it was a particularly good advert for Christianity, especially as both sides claimed His support. The last 'cathedral' I had visited was the Barkhor in Lhasa, which was also full of banners and statues but at least these were all religious. I know that Tibetan Buddhism has its own history of oppression and violence but there was a lot more evidence of devotion and religious commitment than I found in Hereford, home of the SAS.

Continuing on my way, I had more evidence of senility when I rode past the junction with the A466 which leads straight to Monmouth, and carried on down the busy A49, which not only added a few miles to the journey, but decanted me on to the even busier A40, a big frightening dual carriageway with spectacular glimpses of Symonds Yat, a limestone crag perched high on the side of the narrow Wye Valley, which I entered after passing through the old garrison town of Monmouth.

There is something definitely creepy about the Wye Valley, where it cuts through the Forest of Dean. It always seems a dark and gloomy spot, even on a sunny day and I always feel that I am entering an alien land. Despite this, I have many happy memories of evenings spent climbing on its various crags, Wintour's Leap, Windcliffe, Symonds Yat itself and my own favourite, Shorncliffe, buried in impenetrable woodland near Tintern Abbey. It always seemed to be a minor miracle finding it at all, but in my last years of lecturing at Bristol I had many summer evenings climbing with friends.

My feelings about the lower Wye Valley weren't exactly helped when I stopped at a village store, where the newsagent's board proclaimed a brutal family murder in what proved to be the self-same village. Everyone in the shop was talking about it and I felt more of an intruder than normal. When I got to Tintern Abbey I assumed there would be a big campsite but there didn't appear to be anything at all. Eventually, I was told that if I went to the old disused station, now a visitors' centre, there was a field that I could use. And so, for the derisory sum of three pounds, I was directed to an idyllic little glade ('field' was a huge exaggeration) where I could pitch a tent. The station had a washroom and toilet and when the last of the trippers had left it was very peaceful. I decided to cycle the mile or so to the pub immediately opposite the ruins of the abbey, which brought back even more memories of climbing evenings on Shorncliffe before grabbing a quick pint and driving back across the Severn Bridge to Bristol.

Now I was on my own and the only company I had were a couple of surly locals and a coach party of Americans. Most of them were elderly couples but there was one stunning middle-aged woman on her own, reading a thick guidebook. I was convinced that she had been recently widowed; she looked so desperately lonely and insecure. But she was sitting with two couples who were talking to her whenever she looked up and, as usual, I could think of no way of intruding into their conversation. In any case, a portly, middle-aged gent in grubby shorts and a sweaty T-shirt was hardly alluring. But I wished I knew her story. Maybe I was completely wrong and she was a mother of four healthy teenagers taking time off from a husband who doted on her, but somehow I don't think so. When they left the pub and re-boarded their coach, I rode pensively back to my little field.

I awoke smiling as, for no reason I could understand, a memory surfaced. When Joe Simpson had recovered from his epic accident in Peru and written his bestselling book *Touching the Void*, he had put himself through two or three years of intensive physiotherapy and regular rock-climbing (including quite a lot with me in Cornwall). To prove to himself that he was still able to perform on big mountains, he had gone on an expedition to Ama Dablam, the beautiful wedge-shaped summit near Tengboche Monastery on the way to Everest. He had returned successful with fellow Sheffield climber Richard Haszko and gone straight to the Byron pub for a celebration pint. As he entered he was limping quite badly and said that his leg had given him a lot of pain. Richard sat silently for about twenty minutes and then a huge grin spread over his face as he announced: 'I've come from Ama Dablam with a bad knee on my Joe.' What reminded me of the atrocious pun I have no idea, but it still made me laugh out loud.

A big day had dawned. Today I would arrive in Bristol. I would at last be in the West Country, and for the next couple of days I would be amongst friends. It was another scorcher, and the morning started with a long hill climb up from Tintern Abbey, out of the Wye Valley and then down to Chepstow Racecourse. The hill was nowhere near as bad as I remembered – perhaps I was getting fit at last? At the top I was rewarded by a distant view of the old Severn Bridge with the Promised Land of Avon and Somerset in the blue distance. I wasn't quite sure how to get to the bridge. I knew there was a cycle- and pedestrian way across but the traffic was all on the M48 motorway. However, a well-sign-posted set of paths from the outskirts of Chepstow led me onto the clean lines of the bridge, which was far more impressive to cross on a bike than in a car.

At Aust, on the Bristol side, I stopped at what is now unimagi-natively called Severn View Services and celebrated with a bottle of fizzy water. I had noticed some strange anomalies about fizzy water since I started the ride. In north-west Scotland I had drunk lots of Buxton Water, now I was drinking Highland Spring. It did seem slightly odd that lorryloads of the stuff were presumably criss-crossing the country, all tasting, as far as I could tell, absolutely identical. Why did they have to be driven such vast distances? (Or was it perhaps just the labels that travelled? Surely not.)

Instead of going directly into Bristol, I chose to go a slightly longer route by cycling down to Avonmouth and then along the A4 through the Avon Gorge and under the Suspension Bridge. This was, I admit, for sentimental reasons, though it was also completely flat. It gave me a good view of the Second Severn Crossing. The new bridge looks like a couple of huge catamarans moored across the Severn – very impressive but I don't under-stand why the old bridge is no longer the M4 and the new bridge is. Avonmouth is a dirty place, full of wind-blown streets, anony-mous warehouses and poisonous emissions belching from factory chimneys. On a hot day you can imagine slowly dissolving into a puddle of fatty acid, but when I hit the A4 and cycled alongside the river there was an ebb tide and the characteristic Avon Gorge smell of sewage mingled with the fumes from the Rio Tinto Zinc smelter. It wasn't perhaps the most romantic way of entering Bristol but it was worth it for me as I was soon cycling down memory lane, a.k.a. the A4.

The first Gorge landmarks, the Unknown Walls and Unknown Buttress, with their characteristic yellow rock, soon hove into sight, bringing back images of baking sweaty summer evenings climbing after college and racing the setting sun as it sank over the Bristol Channel and the shadows crept up the cliff. The climbs finish on the Downs and often it is possible for a relieved leader still to have enough rope to make it to an ice cream van before belaying his overheated second up the final pitch.

Beyond Unknown Buttress are the Sea Walls. I'd had many pleasant evenings here. Half a mile further on is the centrepiece of the Gorge, Main Wall. Riding slowly past, I could pick out the lines of old favourites, Lich Gates, Pink Wall Traverse, Maltravers and the classic Bonington route, the strangely named Malbogies. It had been my favourite route in the Gorge and I had done it many times, sometimes with visiting luminaries like Henry Barber and Doug Scott, and with Chris himself who, typically, was unable to remember where it went. Then comes the main area, full of old classics like Piton Route, Central Buttress and the delicate lines on Morning Slab. The first time I ever climbed in the Gorge was in 1962 – nearly forty years ago. I had hitched down from London to meet a friend from Oxford University, done a climb called Dawn Walk, and hitched back again. In those pre-motorway days it had taken most of the night to get back to my parents' house in Ealing.

I rode under the Suspension Bridge and cycled on, past another Brunell monument, the SS *Great Britain* berthed in the old docks, and arrived in the centre of Bristol. I knew that two of my old friends from college days were away, but a more recent friend was working at Stanford's book shop. She is a young and talented writer called Kay Dowling who keeps me amused with a series of hilarious ribald letters that, when she becomes famous, I will publish and make a fortune from. As soon as the shop closed we went for a pint or two and had a pizza in a restaurant in King Street, amongst Bristol's oldest and most famous pubs. Although I have always had mixed feelings about my long lecturing career in Bristol, I always enjoyed the vaguely Treasure Islandish, seafaring atmosphere of the old city. Then we bought a couple of bottles of wine and went back to her little house in Bedminster when it was still hot enough to sit outside in the backyard until, full of wine, pizza and conversation, I succumbed to sleep.

The following morning was a Saturday and Kay left early for work. I pottered around and had coffee outside in the sun, enjoying a leisurely start to the day, because I knew I only had to ride a few miles down the road. I was going to stay a couple of nights with an ex-girlfriend, Cass, and her new partner, Brian. They lived in the little village of Congresbury which is well on the way to Weston-Super-Mare. As I rode out into the Somerset countryside I definitely felt that I was making a start on the last leg of my journey. I didn't want to get too excited because I knew I was still four or five days away from my destination and, depending on where that was, it might be more.

Hang on, I hear you say, surely he knows where he's going by now? Well, yes and no. Because I had started by riding up to Muckle Flugga and never felt remotely as though I was doing an End-to-End, I was reluctant to finish at Land's End. I felt that the Lizard, the most southerly point on mainland Britain, was more appropriate. Though, of course, if you are being pedantic, someone who insists on starting from Shetland should end on Jersey. But I'd been there and it was an expensive place to get to. So the Lizard it was. However, I would then have to ride on to Land's End after that because I had arranged to meet most of the Old Spice Girls, plus Geoff Birtles, at Trevedra Farm campsite, near Sennen Cove. Geoff wanted to do a climb with me at Land's End itself to celebrate, so I had spent the last couple of days deciding what to do. I really wanted to finish as I had started, by myself. In the end, I decided to compromise and have both a private and a public occasion. Once I had sorted out this not very difficult decision, I felt much happier.

14

The Last Fold of the Map

I spent Sunday sitting in Cass and Brian's garden while my hangover from the night before receded, watching my washing dry. This included my tent, for some time in the last week I must have pitched it on something quite disgusting or, alternatively, an animal must have mistaken it for a public toilet. Either way it dried out not smelling of roses, and the thought of spending the next few nights in it was now quite tolerable. Cass had been persuaded that her washing machine had suffered no permanent damage, and we drank wine in the afternoon. I was relaxed, the weather was holding and, what's more, the wind was actually coming from the east. I had always dreaded the last lap from Bristol, for I assumed I would be travelling directly into the prevailing wind. Could it be that for once I was going to get a lucky break?

Before I left, I did some more map reading. I had a vivid memory of driving back from holiday in Cornwall last year, and seeing what I presumed were End-to-Enders cycling along the interminable dual carriageways of the A30, battling against heavy wind and rain. I had no intention of using the A30 except for the last few miles from Penzance, but should I go along the north coast of Devon and Cornwall, or south of Dartmoor via Plymouth, Liskeard and Bodmin? In the end I decided on the north coast option. Brian, who hails from Devon, gave me a funny look but said nothing. Cass, who had only seen me riding a bike once, many

years ago, in Bristol, and hadn't stopped laughing since, didn't seem to think I would make it past Weston-Super-Mare, despite the knowledge that I had ridden from some far off place up north even beyond Sheffield. Geography, I have to say, was not her strongest point.

In the morning I reluctantly dragged myself away. As I left, Cass had a not very original idea. 'At least it's all downhill from here.' I realised, as I eased myself back into the rhythm of pedalling, that I had nearly had enough. The next section, via Weston to Bridgwater, was flat and unmemorable and the campsite was a kind of minor Butlin's, with a shop, boating ponds and children's games areas, which charged me the same rate as for a car, a frame tent and two adults. The Somerset Levels were behind me now and, looking south, I could see the blue Quantock Hills. Ahead was Exmoor, which was unavoidable as the great rolling hills and moors do not sweep gently down to sea level as they should, but are sliced off abruptly in a long series of huge rotten cliffs and steep wooded hillsides. This gives interesting road-building problems, which, if I hadn't been suffering from both short- and long-term memory loss, I would have avoided. Instead, I naively decided that I would follow the A39 to Lynmouth. In so doing I gave myself the worst hills of the entire journey, far, far, worse than anything I had ridden in Scotland or the Lakes. The day marked the beginning of the awful realisation that from here to the Lizard would be no pushover and might be a little, or not so little, endurance test in its own right.

I stopped for lunch in Minehead and for the first time since the Arran ferry to Ardrossan I was deeply into holiday territory. Nothing wrong with that, but I did feel isolated cycling through the hordes of holidaymakers. I wasn't feeling particularly sorry for myself, nor was I feeling superior or condescending. Travelling alone cocoons you more than you realise until your small world is challenged. I just felt that I had little in common with the families, the children, the pensioners and the coach parties. What they were doing wouldn't be my choice and I'm quite certain what I was doing wouldn't be theirs. I was quite relieved to resume my solitary journey and try and sink into my afternoon trance.

Which I could have done quite successfully had it not been for Porlock Hill. Looking at my map as I write these words, I am frankly baffled as to why I should have chosen this route. I descended this ridiculously steep incline, only to have to GOAP within yards of the start of the far side. I have never had to push my bike up anything as steep, and several times I had to reverse it into the dry stone wall to stop it escaping as I slumped to rest my aching legs. It went on and on, and on and on. I couldn't believe that any hill could gain so much height at such an angle, and go on for so long. At one point the angle eased off considerably and I remounted. But I was deceived – it was still far too steep to pedal even in the lowest granny gear, and after only a few yards I wobbled to a halt. I remembered Brian's raised eyebrow when I had told him of my intended route, and realised all too clearly why.

When I could get back on the bike, the road led inexorably on uphill for another mile or so. It was a mystery how I could have gained so much height (it felt like about 15,000 feet, higher than Mont Blanc) yet still be so close to the sea. It was an unanswered question all the way from here to Land's End. Colossal uphill stretches led to the top of insignificant hills. Had the road-builders excavated the valley bottoms to well below sea level? And why didn't it seem to be going downhill any more? At the end of the afternoon I did at last descend to Lynmouth where once again I was faced with a monumental hill to escape. Abruptly I marched straight to the first modest hotel I could see and booked in for the night and for an evening meal as well. It was not cheap but I was determined to enjoy it. In fact, it was the only night in the last lap that I didn't spend in the tent (which is just another way of trying to justify it).

Tony and Linda Mears run East Lyn House. They were both enormously friendly and helpful and I was waited on hand and foot. They were the kind of people who should run every hotel and bed and breakfast in the country, because they obviously liked the job and, more importantly, they liked their guests. All of which couldn't put off the moment when, having lingered over breakfast, I had to start pushing straight away. It wasn't quite as awful as Porlock Hill, but it was an unpleasant start to the day and my legs ached from yesterday's exertions. Quite frankly, I had imagined that by this stage in the proceedings I would be as fit as a butcher's dog and would find every day an effortless performance for a perfectly honed body. The opposite was the case, and my weariness was both mental and physical.

It was on this hill that I made an irritating discovery, though why I hadn't noticed it earlier I couldn't understand. This was simply that when I pushed the Beast slowly uphill the speedometer failed to register, which didn't matter, but neither did the milometer, which did. I had kept a record of all the daily imileages from the start and they were all wrong because they didn't include the GOAPs. How far had I pushed this bloody machine from Muckle Flugga? Ten, twenty, thirty miles or more? Whatever it was, I would only end up with a very approximate total. Not that this mattered in the greater scheme of things, but it didn't make me feel any better.

The weather had reverted to type. I had been pathetically grateful for the following wind, even if it had only been a gentle breeze, but now a fresh westerly blew in my face. It was still warm but huge cumulus clouds were forming and I knew that this would probably be the last fine day. I was aiming to make it as far as Bideford by this evening, which would mean I would actually be in Cornwall some time tomorrow. Once off Exmoor I did find the going marginally easier but I was increasingly reverting to the gritted teeth one-mile-at-time mode of progression that I had used on the first few days in the Shetlands. I stopped for fish and chips in Barnstaple, then in the heat of the afternoon plugged on to Bideford. I was still on the A39 but the volume of traffic had increased and I was becoming more and more neurotic.

Even at the planning stage of the journey I had been haunted by the memory of Dave Cook. I had known Cooky on a casual basis for years. London-based and highly political (he had been secretary of the British Communist Party for many years), Dave had taken off on an epic solo ride to Australia, climbing along the way in every major mountain range he had ridden through. It was a far more ambitious and scary undertaking than mine and he had written a book on his return. Before it was published Dave set out on another big ride, this time around the Mediterranean. In Turkey he had been knocked off his bike, either by a passing lorry or the force of its slipstream. He had been flown back to London in a coma, contracted pneumonia and died. In his book he had frequently compared the dangers of climbing and cycling and described horrifying close encounters with lorries in the Middle East. But he had made the decision not to wear a helmet, which might have made all the difference. As I have said before, I was shamed into using one by my daughters. But I have to confess I rarely wear one for rock-climbing which seems, even to me, to be nonsensical. Perhaps as a result of this ride I will start doing so, not before time.

On the busy road to Bideford I was under few illusions as to the increased safety potential of a helmet. The problem was the ever-growing volume of holiday traffic which seemed to provoke more impetuous stress-ridden driving than normal. In particular, suicidal overtaking manoeuvres were becoming more and more frequent. Whereas I had always been aware of the possibility of being hit in the small of the back by a lorry, or sideswiped by a blind motorist, I now faced the chance of a head-on collision with some demented Mr Toad, attempting to cut a second or two off his journey, at the expense of a decade or two off my life.

I arrived in Bideford, hot and sweaty at the end of a sunny afternoon to be told by the Tourist Information Centre that the nearest campsite was at Westward Ho! Which was back up the hill I'd come down. Somehow a site in a town with an exclamation mark built into its name smacked even more of a Butlin's-style theme park than the one outside Bridgwater. I decided a bit of illicit camping was what was needed and, amazingly quickly, I found an obviously private field on the outskirts of Bideford that wasn't overlooked by any buildings. I found a spot in a secluded corner and got a minor buzz of guilty excitement at trespassing within a mile of the town centre.

Perhaps because of this, I woke early, got away before seven and started on the longest stage of the whole trip, though this was not intentional. As I cycled round a long bend in a dual carriageway a badger suddenly emerged from the grass verge and shuffled across the busy road, almost under my wheels. Miraculously it avoided the cars and lorries as well and ambled away into the undergrowth unscathed. They are strange beasts; I remember one committing suicide on the road from Hathersage up to Stanage by apparently deliberately running under my wheels. I can still recall the sickening thud and wondered why it couldn't have changed course. On another occasion, in the same place, in the middle of the night, I had followed one for about a mile as it plodded along the crown of the narrow road refusing to give way to anyone or anything.

Actually, the presence of so much wildlife on the verges had already given me cause for worry. Rabbits, hares, moles, voles, stoats, weasels and God knows what else live fearlessly in Britain's verges, totally unconcerned by the thundering purveyors of violent death passing inches from their whiskers. Yet the approach of a harmless old gent on a bike made them quite panic-stricken and frequently I saw rabbits jumping like startled hares as I passed by, if you forgive the simile. I felt frustrated that I couldn't sit down and quietly explain to them that the dozens of squashed relatives littering the kerbside had all been victims of their horribly misplaced confidence. Why they should have evolved this way was hard to understand. In less than a hundred years roadside wildlife seemed to be genetically programmed to believe that motor traffic equals safety, despite massive evidence to the contrary.

Pondering this, I headed towards Bude and, to my delight and astonishment, approached a sign that said Cornwall and underneath, for the benefit of those locals who can neither understand English nor know where they are, Kernow. I know bilingual signs are politically correct, but I find them faintly patronising, particularly in Wales, where they merely emphasise the fact that English comes first. But it was definitely time for a photograph, a drink and a rest. Larks sang in the sky, and I allowed myself a nearly-there feeling. Perhaps because of this, I almost unconsciously started pushing the pace and the miles from Bude to Camelford rolled past quickly, until the skies darkened, thunder rumbled and suddenly the heavens opened. By the time I was riding down a dual carriageway towards the little town of Indian Queens it was raining as hard as it had on the road to Caldbeck all those weeks before. The difference was that this time I was in the middle of hurtling traffic: lorries with huge bow waves sloughed past and on one downhill stretch everything was going so fast, including me, that I was frightened enough to get off and tried to shelter behind a road sign. Watching the traffic, I realised just how poor the average driver's judgement is: the road was virtually under water and yet cars were driving nose to tail, almost aquaplaning, in poor visibility, and still doing at least 80 miles an hour.

As I stood there I noticed a path on the opposite side of the road that looked as though it might lead somewhere. Anything was better than where I was and, feeling horribly like this morning's badger, I pushed the bike across the road. Five minutes later I was ensconced in a warm pub in the village of St Columb Major. Thunder crashed, and outside the rain bounced of the pavement. I read *The Times*, drank a pint and waited for pie and chips to be heated in the microwave. Bliss. (Not really.)

At last the sun broke through briefly and I emerged from the pub into a steamy afternoon. My next landmark was to cross the busy A30 at Indian Queens and then follow a very minor road towards Truro. I enjoyed the route-finding for the next few miles, riding round a maze of empty roads skirting the little town with the romantic name that it singularly fails to live up to in reality. On the nearby dual carriageway the holiday traffic droned on. I crossed over a bridge as a lone cyclist pedalled below, heavily laden like myself. The road was effectively a two-lane motorway and he seemed horribly vulnerable. As far as I knew, the rest of my journey would avoid any more dual carriageways, and I pedalled peacefully on my way.

The B3275 is a small road, winding its way through the woods, then following a little valley towards Truro. I was definitely flagging a bit and looking for another secluded camping spot, but there was nothing. I imagined that when I reached the main road into Truro there would be a decent site but I was disappointed again. The rain had drifted away and it was turning into a sunny evening. There was another colossal hill out of Truro, which really took it out of me, and then the road narrowed into a typical Cornish high-hedged lane with homeward-bound commuter traffic mixing with the holidaymakers. I was tired, frightened again and I had had enough. All I wanted was a campsite – anything would do. At last I saw the magic sign and I rode into another of those poncey, over-priced caravan parks that I knew would irritate me beyond belief when I paid the fee. What the hell, I had ridden almost eighty miles and broken the back of Cornwall. All the way from Muckle Flugga, I had got a minor buzz out of turning each fold of the map, and a bigger buzz when I went from one map to another. As I sat outside my tent I realised I was almost on to the last but one fold of all. In fact, as this one included the Lizard, it *was* the last fold as far as I was concerned.

I was almost superstitious about not looking forward to the end of the journey, but I couldn't help feeling little jolts of excitement when it occurred to me that I was in much the same position now as the man I had met in the café at Bettyhill. Now I was near the end I needed to give a bit of thought to the logistics, and decided that the simplest thing to do would be to cycle to Helston, now, I hoped, only a very easy day away. Then, as I had done in the Shetlands, cycle unladen down to the Lizard and back, which should be another easy day. After that it was just a short ride over to Penzance and on to Trevedra Farm and the Old Spice Girls reunion.

After a wonderful hot shower (perhaps these luxury sites aren't so bad after all) I sat outside the tent, benignly surveying the landscape and my fellow campers. A father and son emerged from the tent opposite with tennis racquets and balls and they almost instantly managed to reduce me to silent fury. The father was simply a bully, and a stupid one at that. He intimidated his son straight away and kept up a constant stream of belittling comments as the poor lad struggled to bat the ball back to him. 'Keep your feet STILL!' he kept yelling at the crestfallen child, who attempted to play by obeying possibly the second most useless command you could imagine (the most useless being, of course, 'Keep your eyes SHUT!') As the basis of virtually every ball game is to move your feet to the ball, it was not surprising that the lesson ended in tears. I could hardly bear to watch. I fantasised about the accidental tent fire that might break out in the night, when of course I would make sure that, having murdered the parents, I heroically rescued the son who would, once the secret of moving his feet had been explained, go on to win Wimbledon.

It was a surprisingly cold night and I was woken several times by heavy downpours (which might have foiled any arson attempts). In the morning great black clouds welled up from the west. I was eager to get going, even though it would be a short day, and had a quick brew of coffee, saving breakfast for later. After only a few miles it started raining, just as I spotted a large caravan parked in a lay-by. A sign promised hot meals and a drink. Inside were sundry lorry drivers all devoted to maintaining their cholesterol levels at suicidal levels and I joined in happily. The proprietor was a friendly chap and kept up incessant banter with all the occupants, including me. Unlike everyone else from Muckle Flugga southwards, he warned me that from here to Helston there were hills all the way. The rain drummed on the roof and once again thunder rumbled away in the distance. In the end, I dragged myself away and pressed on into the wind. Another squall passed over and bow waves from passing lorries broke over my head. 'Inland surfing' I called it, deciding there was little point in going to Newquay for the real thing.

Going up one short sharp hill, I was on the verge of dismounting when suddenly I had to. Bloody, bloody hell. Another rear wheel puncture. I stood at the roadside, soaked to the skin, genuinely deeply depressed. I actually thought of riding straight to Penzance and catching a train home. I was totally utterly bored with the whole enterprise. But I couldn't just stand there and in the end I pushed the bike uphill yet again, looking for some shelter, which soon materialised in the form of a clapped out motor repair garage.

I peered round the door at a pair of legs protruding from a jacked up car.

'Excuse me,' I said to them. 'Do you mind if I come in out of the rain and mend a puncture?'

'No problem, you come in.'

The owner of the legs was a ruddy-faced Cornishman with a tanned smiley face. I wheeled in the Beast, took off the panniers, turned the bike upside down and removed the back wheel.

'You come var?' (I apologise for the crude approximation of a Cornish accent.)

'Well,' I said modestly. 'I've ridden all the way from Muckle Flugga Lighthouse in the far north of the Shetlands.'

The news failed to impress him. After a while he enquired, 'You doin' this to raise money for charity?'

I couldn't tell a lie. 'No, I'm doing it because I wanted to.'

There was an even longer pause while I wrestled with the tyre. Then he delivered the knockout blow.

'I 'ope you don't mind me saying this, but I thought, if e's doin' this to lose weight, e's obviously failed.'

It took a couple of seconds for me to register what I'd just heard. Then I fell about laughing – it was either that or punch him. There was just no answer, and anyway it was all too true. But with one sentence, the man had lifted my spirits more than he could have ever guessed, and it gave me something to smile about for the rest of the day. He was also the only person to ask me what I thought about when I was riding, which was such an original question I found it hard to answer. By the time I had mended the puncture and repacked all my kit, I had gone from despair to high good humour and left with the man's final comment ringing in my ears. Unfortunately, his wit failed him at the last fence. 'At least it's all downhill from 'ere.'

Which of course it wasn't and all the way to Helston I could see on my left flatter countryside leading down to the Lizard, but the A394 perversely tackled every hill head on. The success of my next little plan depended on finding a campsite at, or very near, Helston, and for once I wasn't just lucky, I hit gold. When I got there and enquired where the nearest campsite was, I was directed to Lower Nansloe Farm, just outside Helston. As I rode down the farm track to the campsite, I had yet another puncture but managed to pump the tyre up hard enough to make it to an idyllic site in a small field, next to secluded farm buildings and surrounded by woods. There was only space for a few tents, not that it mattered because there was nobody else there. Margaret Rowe, who ran it, made me feel welcome. Once again the heavy squalls had passed over and the late afternoon sun was drying out both the grass, and my tent, still wet from last night's rain. I removed the back wheel and repaired the new puncture but I realised as I did so that I had lost more spokes and both the tyres were now so worn that I could see the inner canvas beginning to show through. At least tomorrow I would ride down to the Lizard unladen. But I was slightly worried that the back wheel might collapse completely which, so near the end, would be irritating to say the least.

In the morning the tyre was still hard, and I left the tent and all its squalor for the run down to the Lizard. It was a beautiful day with hardly a cloud in the sky. Once out of Helston, the road flattened out and I cycled the eleven miles in less than an hour. The Lizard hasn't been ruined to quite the same extent as Land's End, but it is still a tourist honey pot. I rode through a little village with its myriad cafés and gift shops and cycled down the steep path to Lizard Point itself. It was hard to feel particularly triumphant, or indeed particularly anything, for I was in the company of dozens of holidaymakers for whom the Lizard was another place to visit for a postcard, a pasty and a cream tea. I pushed the bike as far down the path as I could until I reached a secluded spot where I couldn't get it any further. It was low tide and below me a reef of rocks ran out to a calm sea. I sat in the sunshine and tried to sort out my thoughts.

It seemed a long time and a long way from Muckle Flugga, but that was scarcely a revelation. I had expected to feel very emotional, but apart from mild relief that I had done what I had set out to do, there was nothing much to report. I took a self-portrait on my little camera, as I had done at Muckle Flugga. This proved, if nothing else, that I hadn't lost any weight. (In fact, I found out when I got home, I'd managed to put on a couple of kilos.) After a while, I pushed the bike back up to the village. Then I did celebrate a bit with a visit to the Most Famous Cornish Pasty Shop in Cornwall (as seen on TV), followed by a pint. Then I cycled back to Helston.

On the way back, I had an extraordinary memory recall. When I had first gone to Art College at the tender age of sixteen, I had hitchhiked down to Kynance Cove, near the Lizard, with a sketchbook and a pathetically useless tent. I had spent about three days in the rain on my own, drawing and imagining I was living the life of a solitary genius. In fact, I had become desperately homesick and on the fourth day I returned to Helston. My clearest memory is that the first car that stopped for me was a Jaguar, and it took me all the way to the North Circular Road, dropping me about ten minutes' walk from my home in West Ealing. It was one of the best lifts I ever had in what would prove to be a long and eventful hitching career. I don't suppose I had thought about this little escapade for about thirty years and was amazed at how clearly the details came back to me: I could remember the sketchbook exactly, and the wholly inadequate drawings I had done. Another vivid memory was of going to a shop after two days and suddenly realising that I had completely lost my voice surviving in the wet tent and pitiful sleeping bag with no Lilo or sleeping mat. I had an absurd desire to go back in time and tell the sixteen-year-old that forty years later he would still be camping on his own near the Lizard. (And, incidentally, producing another couple of inadequate drawings in a sketchbook.)

It was a beautiful late afternoon when I returned to Nansloe Farm. A family had arrived with a couple of children and this time I watched them all happily playing football together. Mrs Rowe had told them what I had done and to my embarrassment the children came over to congratulate me, which *did* make me feel quite emotional. I cooked what I hoped would be my penultimate chicken curry and had my normal post-prandial coffee and whisky as the light faded. At last I began to feel a glow of fulfilment, which could of course have been the whisky. Strangely, however hard I tried, I found it almost impossible to relive the trip; the memories would doubtless release themselves in time, but I was so used to living in the present and thinking about the next day that I couldn't recall any more than a few fragments of the last couple of months. These included the first night's camping at Mavis Grind, the crash in Shap village and the welcome in Sheffield. Just about everything else seemed to have been erased, which didn't bode terribly well for the book. If my memory didn't improve it would only be about three pages long. One thought occurred to me as I went to sleep; one day, if ever I managed to find another love in my life, it might be fun to repeat the journey in a car, staying only at all the best places. (Thinking about it now, I'm sure this would be a recipe for certain disaster. Anyone forced to listen to me pompously recounting the minutiae of the journey would probably be driven mad. It would be a lot more sensible to simply give her a copy of the book to read and take her on a package holiday to somewhere hot. It would probably be cheaper as well).

The last morning of the ride. All I had to do was pedal the fifteen miles or so to Penzance, then just another seven or eight to Trevedra Farm. It was not much harder than yesterday, but psychologically I felt drained. I really felt I had finished the ride and was only doing the last bit to please the Old Spice Girls, who were due to arrive any day, and Geoff Birtles, who was determined that I should do a climb at Land's End. But my heart wasn't in it until I cycled the last couple of miles into Penzance and joined the A30 at last. Suddenly I realised that it *was* nearly over. I stopped in the town centre and found (on a Sunday) enough shops open to buy food for the evening, a beach towel(!) and a bottle of celebratory wine. I rode out on the familiar Land's End road. For the last time I crawled up long hills, seemingly with no corresponding downhills. For the last time I told myself to take it bit by bit. But, to my growing amazement, I was now being urged on by passing cars that hooted or wound their windows down and shouted encouragement. A cyclist coming the other way yelled, 'You can do it!' Another one, clearly an End-to-Ender who had just started, looked at me with a look I understood. I knew what he was thinking. Two portly gentlemen came jogging towards me, part of an End-to-End relay. They looked shattered after only five miles but had the breath to congratulate me.

All of which was a bit embarrassing for I wasn't actually going to Land's End. Not today anyway.

OLDER, NO WISER, AND CERTAINLY NO THINNER

15

A Land's End Experience

Trevedra Farm campsite lies under Crows-en-Wra hill and about a mile from Land's End airport where light aircraft take off every few minutes to take holidaymakers for a view of the cliff-top scenery. Jean Nicholas runs it and I have been going there nearly every summer for over thirty years. So when I turned off the A30 and checked in I knew she wouldn't be surprised to see me, only the means by which I arrived. I hoped she might raise an eyebrow when I told her where I'd come from, but she took it in her stride. I booked in for a week and immediately found I had lost my wallet, this time for real. And it had happened just as I was about to celebrate. Oh, bugger, bugger, bugger. I knew almost for certain that I had left the bloody thing in the off-licence in Penzance, full of money I'd just got from a cash machine. I went into the phone box next to the campsite shop and started ploughing through the battered Yellow Pages, cursing my stupidity. I cancelled my credit card and, more in hope than expectation, for it was five p.m. on a Sunday after-noon, started dialling the numbers of off-licences in Penzance. To my joy I hit the right one straightaway. Yes, they had got the wallet. Yes, the money was still there, as was the by now useless credit card. Thank God for that. But it wasn't quite the way I had imagined finishing the ride.

I put my little tent up for the last time and unpacked the panniers. Just as I had finished, a friend, Ken Wrigley, arrived from Sheffield.

I vaguely knew he might be coming down for a few days and was delighted to see him, even more delighted when he told me he had been given a load of gear by Geoff Birtles to give me. This was my own kit bag containing my Phoenix three-man tent, spare clothes and, let joy be unconfined, a couple of pillows to use, instead of my fibre pile jacket and a pannier which had sufficed so far. Suddenly the day took on a rosy glow. Most of the Old Spice Girls would be arriving tomorrow, as would Geoff himself, as well as Gemma, whose school had broken up for the summer holidays. Then I really would feel as though I'd done it.

Two days later, with the whole entourage present and correct, it was time to stage the grand finale. Late in the afternoon I pedalled, unladen, the last couple of miles to the ghastly entrance to the even ghastlier Land's End Experience, or whatever it is called. A notice directed End-to-Enders to sign in for their certificate. I curled my lip disdainfully at it and pushed on through the crowds, past the wrecked schooner, the plastic dinosaurs and all the other crap that seemed to be designed to distract the public from the reason they had come here in the first place. I found the signpost which announced that New York was 3,147 miles away and John O'Groats was 874. Which reminded me to check on my now meaningless mileage, which stood at 1,564 miles. So I decided to round it up to 1,600, which felt about right.

The signpost is situated conveniently close to the hotel with its all-day bar and I had a pint while I waited for the others to arrive. Geoff turned up with a small mountain of climbing gear and we put on our rock boots and harnesses. Then, feeling rather foolish in front of the seething coach parties, we clanked, flat-footed, across to the top of the cliff and descended a wide grassy gully to the foot of the appropriately named Land's End Long Climb. Ken Wrigley, himself an accomplished climber, had been press-ganged into being the official photographer for the day and started looking for suitable vantage points.

Our presence at Land's End had its history. It was here in 1983 that I had finished my '100 Climbs in Ten Days' charity climb, with Phil Kershaw, another good friend from Sheffield. In 1975 Geoff, together with his regular climbing partner Tom Proctor, had climbed a wonderful new route called Yankee Doodle. Locals swore that the superb jamming crack hadn't existed before the first ascent. This was seen by Geoff and Tom as an imaginative excuse for their not having climbed it themselves. I did the route a few years later with Phil and not long afterwards the whole buttress collapsed into the Atlantic, which gave the locals' theory a certain amount of credence. When Geoff and Tom climbed Yankee Doodle it was probably the hardest route at Land's End. Now we were both back for the first time since our respective ascents to climb the easiest route on the cliffs.

The Long Climb is made up of about six very short pitches. (The whole route is not more than 200 feet long.) Each gives a short sharp problem and each ends on big interconnecting ledges that make the whole climb unserious, for it is possible to avoid almost every difficulty and still claim to have done the route. It certainly enabled Ken to dart to and fro and record our progress. Even though the climbing was not particularly difficult, it was strenuous and surprisingly awkward, though some of that in my case was due to climbing virtually one-handed. Geoff, who has always been a highly talented climber, made light work of it, but, aware of the fact that he was belaying an overweight one-armed geriatric, he took his time in rigging bombproof stances.

Consequently, by the time we had pulled out onto the flat top of the last buttress, we were not given an ecstatic welcome from the Old Spice Girls. They claimed to be cold and fed up but, as they were sitting in a warm pub and had been more than adequately refreshed, their complaints lacked conviction. I felt that they were simply indulging in a bit of role-playing, which dated from the days in our youth when we would probably have been hours, if not days, late.

So it was finished, done and dusted. Honour was satisfied. I'd been to Land's End to round the journey off. I was touched and surprised at the warmth and generosity of the congratulations, not just from the Old Spice Girls, Gemma, Geoff and Ken, but subsequently from so many friends around the country. I only found out later that many of them had severe doubts that I would complete the ride. Though, as far as I'm aware, nobody placed any bets one way or the other.

Cycling back in the evening light to Trevedra Farm for the last time, I resolved that I wouldn't get on the Beast again, at least not on this trip. I certainly didn't have the feeling, experienced by many lone travellers, of wanting to carry on and do it all again. But I did want a few more moments on my own, and later that night when everyone had gone to bed I left my tent and walked through the campsite and down the steep path to Whitesand Bay.

Like so many places I had visited in the last months this one held its memories: climbing with Paul Nunn and Don Whillans, of Cass and my children when they were young, of Joe Simpson when he came down here with his girlfriend Jackie, of student field trips from Bristol, of Mike Richardson when we were filming for *Tracks*, of Hilary Nunn, the missing Old Spice Girl still to arrive at Trevedra. What fabulous times we had had, and were still having. It was just different now, and would inevitably change again. I realised that the ride had really been about acceptance, of learning, at last, that you can't always get what you want, but if you try sometimes, you just might find you get what you need. A pity Mick Jagger had already penned these words of wisdom in 1969. I strolled back through the sleeping campsite. I had managed to have an adventure without using my passport. I wondered what and where the next one would be. And with whom, for, although Mac was probably right – I *am* a persistant old bugger – I don't think I am a natural solo traveller. Whatever diversions the future may bring, it would be nice to share them with someone else. Because, despite having been told it so often, I don't really want it to be downhill all the way.

Index

Figures in italics refer to illustrations.

These are the questions to which you already know the answers:

a) Are you doing this for charity?

b) Did you do much training?

c) What is your average daily mileage?

d) How much weight have you lost?

e) Never mind it's all downhill, isn't it?